The Names of the Qur'anic Chapters

Their Origins and Meanings

Shetha Al-Dargazelli

Luna Plena Publishing Birmingham

Production Reference: 1260611

Published by:
Luna Plena Publishing
Birmingham, UK.
www.lunaplenapub.com

ISBN 978-1-906342-08-1

Cover design by:
Mawlid Design
www.mawliddesign.com

Cover image:
The octagonal star is formed by the Arabic names of the 114 chapters of the Qur'an.

About the Author

Shetha Al-Dargazelli is a British scholar who was born in Baghdad, Iraq. She graduated from the Physics Department, College of Sciences, Baghdad University, where she obtained also her M.Sc. in Nuclear Physics. She obtained a PhD in Elementary Particle Physics from the Physics Department, Durham University, UK.

Dr Al-Dargazelli taught at Universities in Iraq where she was appointed professor in 1991. She moved with her husband Dr Louay Fatoohi to the United Kingdom in 1992, where she worked at Durham University and Aston University.

She has published several books, including four university Physics textbooks, one book on Sufism, and another on the status of woman in Islam. She has also translated with Louay the book *Purification of the Mind* (*Jilā' Al-Khāṭir*) by the Sufi Shaikh 'Abd Al-Qādir Al-Jilānī.

Her most recent book is *The Mystery of Israel in Ancient Egypt: The Exodus in the Qur'an, the Old Testament, Archaeological Finds, and Historical Sources*, which she co-authored with her husband. She published over thirty scientific papers in refereed scientific journals. And more than 30 scientific articles in established Arabic cultural and refereed journals.

She has given many talks in the UK and abroad about women in Islam and the spiritual dimensions of Islam.

Currently she teaches at an Islamic College in Birmingham/ UK.

And He taught Adam all of the names.

(Qur’an, 2.31)

Contents

It is the knowledgeable among
Allah’s servants who fear Him.

(Qur’an, 35.28)

Preface

It is very pleasing to see the large amount of literature dedicated to Qur'anic studies from Muslim and non-Muslim scholars all over the world. The more studies we see the more wonders we find in this holy book of Allah. It is narrated that 'Alī bin Abī Ṭālib said that he heard the Prophet say that "Its wonders (the Qur'an) are endless" (*Tirmidhī 2906*, Book 48: Ḥadīth 14).

This book studies the names of the chapters of the Holy Qur'an. It explains the reason behind giving each chapter its name and tries to identify naming patterns. It is divided into two main parts. The first contains seven chapters each of which focuses on certain aspects of the subject; the second, which is Chapter 8, analyses the name of each of the 114 Qur'anic chapters. Let's briefly review the content of the book.

Scholars have developed a number of classification systems for the chapters of the Qur'an. One such system is based on the length of the chapters, where the number of verses is used to calculate the length of the chapter. In contrast to this traditional system, a new system in which the chapter length is determined by the number of words instead is presented in **Chapter 1**. In **Chapter 2** the question of who named the chapters is discussed. **Chapter 3** presents the chapters with two names. **Chapter 4** deals with the Qur'anic origin of the names, while the locations of the names in the Qur'anic chapters are given in **Chapter 5**. **Chapter 6** deals with other characteristics of the names of the chapters, namely the number of letters.

In **Chapter 7** a new system for categorizing the

meanings of the names of the chapter is presented. **Chapter 8** presents the name of each chapter and the verse it occurs in. Finally, **Chapter 9** summarizes the findings of this work.

I am hoping that this work will make a modest contribution to the large volume of literature dedicated to Islamic and Qur'anic studies. I ask Allah for forgiveness for any mistake that I have made.

I would like to add that without the help and encouragement of my husband Louay Fatoohi this work would not have seen the light.

Birmingham/ UK
Rajab 1432 / June 2011

1

The Qur'an

The Holy Qur'an, the sacred book of Islam, was revealed in Arabic to Prophet Muḥammad (peace be upon him). Its first verses were revealed in 610 CE and its revelation was completed over 22 years. The Arabic technical term for the piecemeal revelation of the Qur'an is *munajjam* – a word that means "scattered-stars-like."

In the first twelve years of the revelation, the Prophet was living in Mecca. Mounting persecution then forced him to immigrate to Yathrib which became known as *al-Madīnh al-Munawwarah* (The illuminated city), or Medina for brief, after the Prophet's arrival. Following his immigration or *Hijrah*, the Prophet lived ten years in Medina until his death in 632 CE.

Most Muslim scholars think that the first verses (*āyahs*) of the Qur'an that were revealed are the following (Fatoohi, 2010a):

> Read [O Muḥammad!] in the name of your Lord who created (96.1) — created man from a clot. (96.2) Read, and your Lord is the most honorable (96.3) who taught with the pen (96.4) — taught man what he knew not. (96.5)

The chapter (*sūrah*) that was revealed last, as agreed by most Muslim scholars, is 110. As to which verse was revealed last, scholars have disagreed (Fatoohi, 2010b). The various claims identifying the first and last verses were discussed in Fatoohi's articles (Fatoohi, 2010a and 2010b).

The 114 Qur'anic chapters contain 6236 verses. Depending on its length, each chapter includes one theme or more. The verses were arranged in each chapter by the Prophet as inspired and commanded by Allah (glorious and high is He). There are many *ḥadīths* (Prophetic sayings) that confirm this. For instance, Prophet Muḥammad is reported to have said: "Gabriel (peace be upon him) has come and ordered me to put this verse in this position of this chapter," referring to verse 90 of chapter 16 (*Musnad Aḥmad*, Ḥadīth 'Uthmān bin Abī al-'Āṣ). The fact that it was the Prophet who ordered the verses in each chapter is accepted by both old (e.g. Suyūṭī, pp. 57-62) and the modern scholars (e.g. Zarqānī, pp. 244-245; Qaṭṭān, pp. 140-141).

The beginning of each chapter is marked by the expression *Bismillāhi ar-Raḥmān ar-Raḥīm* (In the name of Allah the Merciful the Compassionate), also known as the *Basmalah*. The only exception to this rule is chapter 9 which is called *at-Tawbah* (The Repentance).

There are a number of explanations for this exception, with the following two being the most agreed upon by Muslim scholars. **First**, as chapter 9 was revealed late in Medina after the battle of Tabūk (9 H / 630 CE), it is considered as a continuation of chapter 8. **Second**, the disbelievers and hypocrites who are addressed angrily in the first verse of this chapter are not eligible for God's mercy and compassion that is represented by the *Basmalah*. We'll see later that the latter explanation is more plausible.

Despite the fact that the *Basmalah* is missing from chapter 9, the existence of a *Basmalah* in verse 18 of chapter 27 makes the total number of *Basmalahs* in the Qur'an equal to the number of its chapters. It is worth mentioning that the *Basmalah* in the first chapter (al-Fātiḥah / the Opening), unlike the case in the other chapters, is part of the chapter and is counted as the first verse.

One system of classifying the Qur'anic chapters is by place of revelation, i.e. before or after Hijrah. A chapter is called Meccan (M) or Medinite ("H" for "Hijrah") depending on whether the majority of its verses were revealed before or after Hijrah. This classification helps in better understanding the Qur'anic verses. Meccan chapters are more poetic in style and are concerned mainly with teaching and clarifying the basics of the faith, whereas Medinite chapters are more focused on establishing the law as the Muslim community continued to grow and an Islamic state was in the making. This difference in emphasis is reflected in the names of the Meccan and Medinite chapters, as we shall later see in Chapter 7. More information about the Meccan and Medinite chapters is presented in Table 1.1.

Table (1.1): A comparison between the number of Meccan and Medinite chapters, verses, words and letters

	Chapters	Verses	Words	Letters
Meccan	86	4,613	47,679	195,205
Medinite	28	1,623	30,104	127,351
Total	114	6,236	77,783	322,556
Ratio (M/H)	3.07	2.84	1.58	1.53

There are three times more Meccan chapters than Medinite ones. But the ratio drops to about 1.5 for the number of words or letters because the average Medinite chapter is significantly longer than the average Meccan, making up around 60% of the Qur'an Meccan. Further relevant statistics are given in Table 1.2.

With the exception of the letters per word, all other averages are higher for the Medinite revelations than the

Meccan ones. In the case of words and letters per chapter, the Medinite figures are about double their Meccan equivalents. With both having the same average number of letters per word, the number of words can be used as an indicator for the length of a verse or a chapter.

Table (1.2): A statistical comparison between the Meccan and Medinite chapters.

Average number	Meccan	Medinite	All
Verses per chapter	54	58	55
Words per chapter	554	1075	682
Words per verse	10	19	12
Letters per chapter	2270	4548	2829
Letters per verse	42	78	52
Letters per word	4	4	4

It must have become already clear that the Qur'anic chapters are of varying lengths. The longest chapter, which is chapter 2 (*al-Baqarah* / the Cow), consists of 286 verses, whereas the shortest consists of 3 verses only. Chapters 108 (*al-Kawthar* / the Abundance), 103 (*al-'Aṣr* / the Time), and 110 (*an-Naṣr* / the Help) have three verses each. Chapter 110 has 19 words and chapter 103 has 14 words, so chapter 108, which has only 10 words, is the shortest chapter.

The length of the chapter is the basis for another categorization system. The classical system consists of four categories, with the fourth category divided into three subcategories. The first category is known as *Ṭīwāl* (long ones) and consists of the seven longest chapters, which include chapters 2-7. The seventh chapter is taken by some scholars to be chapters 8 and 9 combined, i.e. treating them as one chapter, and by others as chapter 10.

The second category includes all chapters consisting of over 100 verses. This group is called *Mi'ūn*, which is a technical term derived from the Arabic word for hundred.

The third category is the *Mathānī* (the repeated ones). These chapters are shorter than the previous two groups and people read them more frequently than the chapters of the first two groups, hence their name.

The forth and last category is the *Mufaṣṣal* (divided ones). This group is named after the large number of *Basmalas* that separate its chapters. Some say that *Qāf* / Arabic Letter Q (chapter 50) is the first chapter of the Mufaṣṣal category, but others say it is *al-Ḥujurāt* / The Apartments (49).

The Mufaṣṣal group is further divided into three subcategories: the longer ones, from 50-78, or 49-85; the middle ones, from 78-93 or 85-98; and the short ones, consisting of the remaining chapters (al-Qaṭṭān pp. 145-6).

Table (1.3): The Classical categorization of chapters by length (number of verses)

<table>
<tr><th>Category</th><th colspan="2">Chapters</th></tr>
<tr><td>Tīwāl (Long ones)</td><td colspan="2">2-9 (considering 8 & 9 as one chapter) or 2-7 and 10</td></tr>
<tr><td>Mi'ūn (Hundreds)</td><td colspan="2">All chapters with more than 100 verses</td></tr>
<tr><td>Mathānī (Repeated ones)</td><td colspan="2">All chapters between Mi'ūn and Mufaṣṣal</td></tr>
<tr><td rowspan="3">Mufaṣṣal (Divided ones)</td><td>Long</td><td>50-77 or 49–84</td></tr>
<tr><td>Middle</td><td>78-92 or 85-97</td></tr>
<tr><td>Short</td><td>93–114 or 98–114</td></tr>
</table>

The classical system, shown in Table (1.3), is approximate rather than accurate. In general, the number of words increases with the number of verses, but there are chapters with a small number of verses yet with a relatively large number of words. For example the 227 verses of chapter 26 have 1322 words, whereas the 111 verses of chapter 17 have 1559 words. So chapter 17 is longer than chapter 26 even though it has less than half the number of verses.

So the number of verses is not an accurate indicator of the length of the chapter. I will, therefore, use a new classification system in which the chapter length is determined by the number of words it contains. The same category names of the classical categorization will be used in the new classification system.

The longest chapters (*Ṭiwāl*) in descending order of number of words (between 6144 and 2506 words or, approximately, 6100-2500) are as follows: 2, 4, 3, 7, 6, 5, and 9. It is worth mentioning that these are also the longest chapters in terms of the number of verses but in a slightly different descending order: 2, 7, 3, 4, 6, 5, and 9.

Chapter 10 is only the 10th in terms of the number of words and the 13th if the number of verses is considered. Chapter 9 has its own name so it cannot be a continuation of chapter 8. So the classical *Ṭiwāl* should be amended, as stated above. Note that chapters 6 and 7 are Meccan and the other five of the *Ṭiwāl* category are Medinite. This is the only category with more Medinite chapters than Meccan.

In the classical classification, the *Mi'ūn* chapters are 17 in total. The range of 1900-1100 words covers 18 chapters in the new system. They are in descending order of length: 16, 11, 10, 12, 17, 18, 28, 33, 24, 26, 8, 20, 22, 40, 21, 39, 27, and 23. Out of the 18, only four — 33, 24, 8, and 22 — are Medinite.

The *Mathānī* may be considered to be the next 20 chapters, which fall in the range of 1000-600 words. These are: 29, 19, 37, 25, 34, 14, 13, 43, 42, 30, 41, 35, 38, 36, 15, 46, 57, 48, 47, and 31. Only four out of the 20 chapters — namely 13, 57, 48, and 47 — are Medinites.

The *Mufaṣṣal* and its three subcategories — long, middle, and short — would then cover the remaining 69 chapters. 15 of the *Mufaṣṣals* are Medinite.

The long subcategory, in the rage 500–200 words, consists of the following 27 chapters in descending order: 45, 58, 59, 56, 55, 32, 60, 51, 49, 50, 44, 54, 53, 67, 52, 68, 65, 69, 72, 66, 64, 76, 74, 70, 71, 61, and 73. Ten out of these 27 chapters are Medinites: 58, 59, 55, 60, 49, 65, 66, 64, 76, and 61.

The middle subcategory may be represented by the range of 190–50 words. Twenty one chapters fall in this subcategory: 77, 63, 78, 79, 62, 83, 75, 89, 90, 85, 84, 81, 98, 88, 90, 82, 92, 87, 96, 86, and 91. Chapters 63, 62, and 98 are Medinite.

The last subcategory — the short chapters — represents the range of 40–10 words. It consists of the following 21 chapters: 93, 100, 101, 95, 99, 1, 104, 102, 97, 107, 94, 105, 109, 111, 114, 110, 106, 113, 103, 112, and 108. Only chapters 99 and 110 are Medinite.

The new classification system accurately groups chapters by their number of words. It is more accurate than the classical system which is based mainly on the number of verses.

Table (1.4): The new classification of chapters by the number of words

	No. of Words	Rounded Range	No. of Chapters
Ṭīwāl	6,144-2,506	6,100-2,500	7
Mi'ūn	1,845-1,051	1,900-1,100	18
Mathānī	982-550	1,000-600	20
Mufaṣṣal			69
Long	488-200	500-200	27
Middle	181-54	190-50	21
Short	40-10	40-10	21

We should note again that chapters in the written Qur'an (*muṣḥaf*) are ordered, in general, by length. This means that they are not listed by chronological order of revelation. I have already pointed out that chapter 96 was the first to be revealed. While scholars have differed on the last chapter that the Prophet received, it is agreed that it was not chapter 114. For more details of the difference between the Qur'an and Muṣḥaf the reader may consult "The difference between Qur'an and Muṣḥaf" by Louay Fatoohi (2010c).

To facilitate its regular reading or memorizing, scholars have suggested various kinds of division of the Qur'an. The first is called "*manāzil*," which is the plural of "*manzil* (station)". There are 7 *manāzil* which enable the recitation of the whole Qur'an in one week. Chapter number 1 is not included as it is considered a preface in this classification. See Table (1.5).

Another kind of division splits the Qur'an into 30 equal parts each of which is known as "*juz'* (part)." For example, to read the whole Qur'an during the fasting month of Ramaḍān, the Muslim can read one part a day.

This is shown in Table (1.5). The fourth column represents the number of pages according to a Muṣḥaf of about 600 pages.

Table (1.5): The division of the Qur'an according to manāzil

Manzil number	Chapter number	Part number	Number of pages of Muṣḥaf
1	2,3,4	1-4	104
2	5-9	5-10	102
3	10-16	11-14	74
4	17-25	15-18	87
5	26-36	19-22	79
6	37-49	23-26	72
7	20-114	27-30	87

Each part (*juz'*) is, in turn, divided into two halves each of which is called *ḥizb*, which may be translated as "section." Finally, each *ḥizb* is divided into four parts each of which is known as *rub'* (quarter). There are, thus, eight *rub's* in a *juz'*. This allows the recitation of one *rub'* in each of the eight *ruk'ahs* (one complete sequence of bowing the body and prostration) in the daily *Tarāwīḥ* prayers during the month of Ramaḍāan.

So the Qur'an has 7 *manāzil*, 30 *juz's*, 60 *ḥizbs*, and 240 *rub's*. These are usually marked on the margins of the printed Qur'an, which is known as the *muṣḥaf*.

We have seen in this chapter that there are a number of different systems for classifying the chapters of the Qur'an. The first is classification by date of revelation. A chapter is called Meccan or Medinite depending on when the majority of its verses were revealed, i.e. before or after *Hijrah*. The second classifies the chapters according by length, using the number of verses. But the number of verses is not an accurate indicator of the length of the chapter. I have presented a new classification system in which the chapter length is determined by the number of words it contains. Another classification system is intended to facilitate the regular reading or memorizing of the Qur'an. In this system, the Qur'an is split into 7 *manāzil*, 30 *juz's*, 60 *ḥizbs*, and 240 *rub's*.

2

The Prophet's Naming of the Qur'anic Chapters

Muslim scholars differentiate between practices derived from the Prophet's sayings and actions and those based on his companions'. The former are called *tawqīf*, meaning they are traceable to the Prophet himself, which in turn means that they were guided by inspiration from God (SWT). They are more known as the "sunnah" or "way of life" of the Prophet. Some of the actions of the companions reflect what they have learned from the Prophet but others reflect their *ijtihād* or "reasoning." When the answer to a question is not found in the Qur'an or Sunnah, Muslims resort to *ijtihād*.

Most Islamic worship rituals, such as the number of prayers per day and the Hajj rituals, are attributed to *tawqīf*, i.e. they are divinely prescribed. The same applies to the order of the verses of the Qur'an, as mentioned earlier. Examples of practices that are derived using *ijtihād* include the addition of signs to the Muṣḥaf to show the reader when to make a short stop and when to continue. There are other issues on which scholars do not agree whether they were divinely commanded or developed by the companions of the Prophet. One such issue is the order of the chapters in the Qur'an (as-Suyūṭī, pp. 62-63; az-Zarqānī, pp. 249-254; al-Qaṭṭān, pp. 142-145).

The majority of Muslim scholars agree that the names of the chapters of the Qur'an were revealed to Prophet

Muḥammad by the Archangel Gabriel. Others think that the Prophet named the chapters and Gabriel approved them. Both views confirm that the names were identified by the Prophet and used during his life. These views, then, consider the identification of the names of the Qur'anic chapters to have been done by *tawqīf.*

There are ḥadīths showing the Prophet referring to various chapters with the names with which they have become known. In one ḥadīth Prophet Muḥammad is reported to have said to 'Umar bin al-Khaṭṭāb: "Does the verse that was revealed in summer at the end of chapter al-Nisā' not suffice you?" (*Ṣaḥīḥ Muslim, Kitāb al-Farā'iḍ, Bāb Mirāth al-Kilālah*). Abū ad-Dardā' reported that the Prophet said: "If anyone learns by heart the first ten verses of the chapter of al-Kahf, he will be protected from ad-Dajjāl (the imposter)" (*Ṣaḥīḥ Muslim*, Kitāb aṣ-Ṣalāht, Bāb Faḍl Surah al-Kahf wa Āyah al-Kūrsī). Another example comes from Ibn Abbās who said that an angel descended from heaven and told the Prophet: "Rejoice in two lights given to you that have not been given to any prophet before you: The Fātīḥah of the Book and the concluding verses of the chapter of al-Baqarah" (*Ṣaḥiḥ Muslim*, Kitāb aṣ-Ṣalāh, Bāb Faḍl al-Fātiḥah wa Khawātīm Sūrah al-Baqarah).

There are also many sayings attributed to companions of the Prophet in which Qur'anic chapters are referred to by their names. For instance, 'Ā'ishah, the wife of the Prophet, is reported to have said: "When the chapters of al-Baqarah and an-Nisā' were revealed, I was with him" (*Ṣaḥīḥ al-Bukhārī*, Kitāb Faḍā'il al-Qur'ān, Bāb Ta'līf al-Qur'ān).

It is a unique aspect of the Holy Qur'an that the names of its chapters came from the Prophet himself. This is not the case in other sacred books. Take, for instance, the Old and New Testaments of the Bible. The names of the Biblical books are conventional, so even those who believe the Bible to be the word of God do not consider the names of these books as part of the revelation. For instance, the name of the book of Genesis is not considered part of the reveled text of that book.

O people! We have created you male and female and made you nations and tribes that you may know one another. The noblest among you in the sight of Allah is the most pious of you. Allah is all-knowing, all-aware.

(Qur’an, 49.13)

3

Chapters with Two Names

There are eight chapters each of which has two names. Of these, chapters 5, 9, 47, 65, and 76 are Medinite.

Table (3.1): The chapters with two names

No.	First Name	Second Name
5	Al-Mā'idah (The Table of Food)	Al-'Uqūd (The Agreements)
9	At-Tawbah (The Repentance)	Al-Barā'ah (The Immunity)
17	Al-Isrā' (The Night Journey)	Bānī Isrā'īl (The Children of Israel)
35	Fāṭir (The Originator [of Creation])	Al-Malā'ikah (The Angels)
40	Ghāfir (The Forgiver)	Al-Mu'min (The Believer)
47	Muḥammad	Al-Qitāl (The Fighting)
65	Aṭ-Ṭalāq (The Divorce)	An-Nisā' aṣ-Ṣughrah or al-Quṣrah (The shorter [chapter of] the Women)
76	Al-Insān (The Human being)	Ad-Dahr (The Time)

Scholars, however, have disagreed about which chapters have a second name. For example, the following five sources, listed in chronological order, have each mentioned the second name of some chapters but not others:

1. Ibn Kathīr (d. 1373): 9, 17, and 47.
2. Pickthall (1875-1936): 9, 17, 35, and 76.
3. Yūsuf 'Alī (1872-1953): 9, 17, 35, 40, and 76.
4. Muṣḥaf al-Madīnah (1984): 35, 40, 47, and 76
5. Al-Ghazālī (1917-1996): 5, 9, 17, 40, 47, and 65.

It is worth mentioning that as-Suyūṭī in his *al-Itqān Fī 'Ulūm al-Qur'ān* (pp. 52-56) mentions all these second names, except that of chapter 76.

The following table shows which chapter has its second name mentioned by each of these sources. The sources are referred to with their numbers above, e.g. Pickthal (SR 2).

Table (3.2): The second chapter names in five sources

No.	SR 1	SR 2	SR 3	SR 4	SR 5
5	N	N	N	N	Y
9	Y	Y	Y	N	Y
17	Y	Y	Y	N	Y
35	N	Y	Y	Y	N
40	N	N	Y	Y	Y
47	Y	N	N	Y	Y
65	N	N	N	N	Y
76	N	Y	Y	Y	N

So there are six chapters that are given two names in three or more of the five quoted references. These are 9, 17, 35, 40, 47, and 76. The second names of chapters 5 and 65 are mentioned by al-Ghazālī only.

Some chapters have also been given descriptive names that differ from their names. For instance, chapter 1, al-Fātiḥah (The Opening [of the Book]), has over 20 descriptive names referring to the benefits of reading it. These include "Ummul Kitāb" (the Essence of the Book) and "ash-Shāfiyah" (the healer) (as-Suyūṭī, pp. 52-53). The second chapter, al-Baqarah (The Cow), is described as "al-Fiṣṭāṭ" (The Tent) and "Sanāmu al-Qur'ān" (The Pinnacle of the Qur'an).

The two longest chapters, al-Baqarah (2) and Āl 'Imrān (3), are called "az-Zahrāwān" (The Two Ever-Flowering). Chapter Yā Sīn (36) is also described as "Qalb al-Qur'ān" (The Heart of the Qur'an). Ar-Raḥmān (55) is also called "'Arūs al-Qur'ān" (The Bride of the Qur'an). The last two chapters, al-Falaq (113) and an-Nās (114), are called al-Mu'awwidhatān (The Two That Protect), and so on. Just to emphasize, these are descriptions not names. For more details on the descriptive names of other chapters the reader may consult *al-Itqān fī 'Ulūm al-Qur'ān* (as-Suyūṭī, pp. 52-57).

It is also common to refer to a chapter using its first verse. For instance, an-Naba' (78) is also called *"Ammā Yatasā'alūn"* (*Ṣaḥīḥ al-Bukhārī, Kitāb Faḍāi'l al-Qur'ān, Bāb Ta'līf al-Qur'ān*). The latter, which means "what are they asking about," is the first two words in the chapter. Similarly, there are seven chapters that start with the two separate letter "*Ḥā' Mīm*," so they are called "Ḥāwamīm," which means "those that start with *Ḥā' Mīm*."

Finally, we should note that certain verses have also been given specific names. For instance, verse 2.255 (or 2.256 also) is called "Āyah al-Kursī" (The Verse of the Chair). Verse 2.282, which is the longest verse in the Qur'an, is known as "Āyah ad-Dayn" (The Verse of Debt). "Āyah al-Mubāhalah" (The Verse of the Prayer of Argument) is how verse 3.61 is known. Verse 24.35 is called "Āyah an-Nūr" (The Verse of Light).

He who does the weight of an atom of good shall see it, and he who does the weight of an atom of evil shall see it.

(Qur'an, 99.7-8)

4

The Qur'anic Origin of the Chapter Names

In terms of their derivation from words in their respective chapters, the names of the Qur'anic chapters may be grouped in three categories.

First, the smallest category contains chapters whose names are not found in exact or derivative form in their chapters. There are only three such chapters: al-Fātiḥah (1), al-Anbiyā' (21), and al-Ikhlāṣ (112). All three are Meccan.

Al-Fātiḥah means "The Opening," and its name is derived from the fact that it is the first chapter in the muṣḥaf.

Al-Anbiyā', which means "The Prophets," is called so because it contains the names of as many as 15 prophets and stories about several of them. This is the largest number of stories about prophets mentioned in a chapter in the Qur'an. The chapter of al-An'ām (6) contains the names of 18 prophets, but only part of the story of the prophet Ibrāhīm is mentioned in this chapter. Unlike the words "al-Fātiḥah" and "al-Ikhlāṣ," which are not found in the Qur'an, the word "al-Anbiyā'" appears several times in various chapters.

The third and last chapter in this category is al-Ikhlāṣ. The name means "The Purity" or "The Exclusiveness." It summarizes the essence of Qur'anic theology, emphasizing the oneness of God and the fact that He has no peer.

The **second** category consists of 11 chapters. These exact names are not found in their respective chapters, but each is a noun derived from a verb found in its chapter.

Table (4.1): The 11 chapters whose names are derived from verbs found in their respective chapters

No	Name	No	Name
17	Al-Isrā'	8	At-Takwīr
32	As-Sajdah	8	Al-Infiṭār
58	Al-Mujādilah	8	Al-Inshiqāq
60	Al-Mumtaḥanah	9	Al-Inshirāḥ
65	Aṭ-Ṭalāq	9	Az-Zalzalah
66	At-Taḥrīm		

Six of these chapters are Meccan (17, 32, 81, 82, 84 and 94). The other five are Medinite.

Third, the name of each of the remaining 100 chapters appears in its **exact form** in its chapter. These chapters can be classified in five subcategories.

The first group consists of four chapters whose names are separate letters at the beginning of their chapters. These are "Ṭā Hā" (20), "Yā Sīn" (36), "Ṣād" (38), and "Qāf" (50). All four are Meccan.

Thirty two chapters make up the second group. The name of each of these appears only once in the Qur'an, i.e. in its chapter. These chapters are listed in Table 4.2. Only six of these 32 chapters are Medinites: 3, 8, 49, 59, 62, and 64. The remaining twenty six are Meccans.

Table (4.2): The 32 chapters whose names appear only once in the Qur'an

No	Name	No	Name
3	Āl 'Imrān	73	Al-Muzzammil
8	Al-Anfāl	74	Al-Muddaththir
15	Al- Ḥijr	77	Al-Mursalāt
16	An-Naḥl	79	An-Nāzi'āt
26	Ash-Shu'arā'	83	Al-Muṭaffifūn
30	Ar-Rūm	93	Aḍ-Ḍuḥā
37	Aṣ-Ṣāffāt	95	Aṭ-Ṭīn
40	Ghāfir	100	Al-'Ādiyāt
42	Ash-Shūrā	103	Al-'Aṣr
45	Al-Jāthiyah	104	Al-Hummazah
46	Al-Aḥqāf	105	Al-Fīl
49	Al-Ḥujurāt	106	Quraish
51	Adh-Dhāriyāt	107	Al-Ma'ūn
59	Al-Ḥashr	108	Al-Kawthar
62	Al-Jumu'ah	111	Al-Masad
64	At-Taghābun	113	Al-Falaq

The third group consists of thirty nine names each of which occurs more than once in the Qur'an but appears last in its specific chapter. I have included al-Baqarah whose name appears only in its chapter. These chapters are listed in Table 4.3.

Table (4.3): The 39 chapters whose names appear last in the Qur'an in those chapters

No	Name	No	Name
2	Al-Baqarah	70	Al-Ma'ārij
5	Al-Mā'idah	71	Nūḥ
7	Al-A'rāf	72	Al-Jinn
13	Ar-Ra'd	75	Al-Qiyāmah
18	Al-Kahf	76	Ad-Dahr
22	Al-Ḥajj	78	An-Naba'
25	Al-Furqān	80	'Abasa

27	An-Naml	85	Al-Burūj
28	Al-Qaṣaṣ	86	Aṭ-Ṭāriq
29	Al-'Ankabūt	88	Al-Ghāshiyah
31	Luqmān	91	Ash-Shams
34	Saba'	96	Al-'Alaq
39	Az-Zumar	97	Al-Qadr
41	Fuṣṣilat	98	Al-Bayyinah
43	Az-Zukhruf	101	Al-Qāri'ah
44	Ad-Dukhān	102	At-Takāthur
57	Al-Ḥadīd	109	Al-Kāfirūn
63	Al-Munāfiqūn	110	An-Naṣr
67	Al-Mulk	114	An-Nās
69	Al-Ḥāqqah		

Eight of these 39 chapters are Medinites, namely 2, 13, 22, 57, 63, 76, 98 and 110. The remaining 31 are all Meccans.

The names of the fourth group of 13 chapters appear in their chapters before they last appear in the Qur'an. In other words, each of these names makes its penultimate appearance in the muṣḥaf in the chapter named after it.

Table (4.4): The name of each of these 13 chapters makes its penultimate appearance in the muṣḥaf in the chapter named after it

No	Name	No	Name
9	At-Tawbah	56	Al-Wāqi'ah
10	Yūnus	68	Al-Qalam
11	Hūd	87	Al-A'lā
12	Yūsuf	89	Al-Fajr
19	Mariam	90	Al-Balad
47	Muḥammad	92	Al-Layl
52	Aṭ-Ṭūr		

There are only two Medinite chapters in this group, namely 9 and 47 and the remaining 11 are Meccan chapters.

The last group of 12 chapters does not belong to any of the above group sand are shown in Table (4.5).

Table (4.5): The names of these chapters do not belong to the above groups

No	Name	No	Name
4	An-Nisā'	35	Fāṭir
6	Al-An'ām	48	Al-Fatḥ
14	Ibrāhīm	53	An-Najm
23	Al-Mū'minūn	54	Al-Qamar
24	An-Nūr	55	Ar-Raḥmān
33	Al-Aḥzāb	61	Aṣ-Ṣaff

Half of these 12 chapters are Meccans, namely 6, 14, 23, 35, 53 and 54.

In this chapter we have seen that there are three categories for classifying the Qur'anic origin of the names of the chapters. The smallest category contains only 3 chapters whose names are not found in exact or derivative form in their chapters. The second category consists of 11 chapters. These exact names are not found in their respective chapters, but each is a noun derived from a verb word in its chapter. Third, the name of each of the remaining 100 chapters appears in its exact form in its chapter.

These 100 chapters were classified into five subcategories. The first group consists of four chapters whose names are separate letters at the beginning of their chapters. Thirty two chapters make up the second group. The name of each of these appears only once in the Qur'an, i.e. in its chapter. The third group consists of thirty nine names each of which occurs a few times in the Qur'an but appears last in its specific chapter. The name of each chapter in the fourth group of 13 chapters also appears more than once in the muṣḥaf but it occurs in it appears once more in a later chapter. The last group of 12 chapters I could not find a specific group for them. Table 4.6 summarizes these results.

Table (4.6): The number of chapters according to the Qur'anic origin of their names

Name's occurrence in the muṣḥaf	Exact	Derived	Total
Not mentioned			3
Derived word		11	11
Exact word		100	100
Letters	4		4
Appears once	32	2	34
Appears last	39	7	46
Appears before the last time (penultimate)	13	1	14
None of the above	12	1	13

5

The Locations of the Names in the Chapters

This chapter examines the locations of the names in their respective chapters. As mentioned in the previous chapter, there are three chapters whose names do not appear in the text of the chapter, so we will be focusing here on the remaining 111 chapters.

There are 64 chapters whose names appear in the first verse. Fifty two of these are Meccans. The Meccan chapters are: 17, 20, 23, 25, 35, 36, 37, 38, 50, 51, 52, 53, 54, 56, 67, 68, 69, 71, 72, 73, 74, 75, 77, 79,80, 81, 82, 83, 84, 85, 86, 87, 88, 89, 90, 91, 92, 93, 94, 95, 97, 100, 101, 102, 103, 104, 105, 106, 108, 109, 113, and 114. The twelve Medinite chapters are: 4, 8, 48, 55, 58, 63, 65, 66, 76, 98, 99, and 110.

One other interesting observation is that in nine cases, the name represents a whole verse in that chapter, i.e. verse 1 is one word. These are Ṭā Hā (20), Yā Sīn (36), aṭ-Ṭūr (52), ar-Raḥmān (55), al-Ḥāqqah (69), al-Fajr (89), aḍ-Ḍuḥā (93), al-Qāri‘ah (101), and al-‘Aṣr (103). Only chapter 55 is Medinite, and the rest are Meccan.

Of the remaining 47 chapters, there are 18 whose names appear in verses 2-10. Twelve other chapters have their names in verses 11-30. The names of the remaining seventeen chapters are found in verse 31-224. Table 5.1 gives the number of chapters in each category of the locations of the chapter name and its percentage of the total number of chapters in the Qur'an.

Table (5.1): The locations of the chapter names

Verse of the name	Number of chapters	Percentage of all chapters
None	3	2.6%
1st	64	56.1%
2nd–10th	18	15.8%
11th–30th	12	10.5%
31st–224th	17	14.9%

While 64 names appear in the first verse of their respective chapters, the names of only two chapters represent the last word in the chapters. These are the two short Meccan chapters of al-Mā'ūn (107.7) and al-Masad (111.5).

So the names of over half of the chapters (56.1%) appear in the first verse and about three quarters (72%) of the chapters appear in the first ten verses.

There are four chapters whose names appear in the last theme of the chapter. These are al-Mā'ida (5.112), ash-Shu'arā' (26.224), az-Zumar (39.71), and al-Jumu'ah (62.9). Chapters 26 and 39 are Meccan while the other two are Medinite.

6

The Number of Letters of the Chapter Names

The twenty eight letters of the Arabic language are classified into two types in terms of articulation. The first is known as the Shamsī (solar) letters. These are 14 consonants that have the same point of articulation with the letter "l" in the Arabic definite article *al* (the). The second type is the Qamarī (lunar) letters. These are 3 vowels and 11 consonants that have different points of articulation with the letter "l".

If the first letter of the word is a solar letter, it assimilates with the letter "l" of the preceding definite article and replaces it in pronunciation. For instance, the name of chapter 91 is written *al-Shams* (The Sun) but is pronounced as *ash-Shams.* This is why these letters are called "shamsī" or "solar." This doubling of the solar consonant letters does not happen with lunar letters. For instance, the name of chapter 54 is written and pronounced as *al-Qamar* (The Moon).

There are 14 solar consonants and 14 lunar letters in Arabic including the three vowels. These are shown in Table 6.1.

Table (6.1): The solar and lunar letters of Arabic

Solar	ن، ل، ظ، ط، ض، ص، ش، س، ز، ر، ذ، د، ث، ت
Lunar	هـ، ي، و، م، ك، ق، ف، غ، ع، خ، ح، ج، ب، ء

The names of only 19 Qur'anic chapters do not contain the definite article *Al* (the). Five of these names start with solar letters, and the other 14 start with lunar letters. Two of these 19 chapters were revealed in the Medina, so 17 are Meccans.

The names of ninety five (or around 83%) chapters start with the definite article. Of these, 69 were revealed in Mecca and the remaining 26 in Medina.

The shortest name of a Qur'anic chapter consists of one letter. There are two such chapters: Ṣād (38) and Qāf (50). Both are Meccan. There are five chapters whose names are two-letter long. These are Ṭa Hā (20), Yā Sīn (36), al-Ḥajj (22), aṣ-Ṣaff (61), and al-Jinn (72). The last three contains the two-letter definite article, but we are not counting these with the number of letters of the name. Chapters 22 and 61 are Medinites.

The longest chapter name consists of 7 letters. There are three names in this category: Āl 'Imrān (3), Ibrāhīm (14) and al-Munāfiqūn (63). Only chapter 14 is Meccan. Again, it seems that Medinite chapters have longer names than the Meccan ones. Table 6.2 categorizes the length of the names of the Qur'anic chapters.

Table (6.2): The frequency of the number of letters of the chapter names excluding the two letters of the definite article

Number of Letters	Frequency
1	2
2	5
3	35
4	28
5	27
6	14
7	3
Total	114

The highest frequency is that for three-letter words followed by four- and then five-letter words. The average number of letters is 4.

Eighty six of the chapter names are in the singular while the remaining 28 names are in the plural. Five of the 28 plural names are Medinite (4, 8, 33, 49 and 63). The majority of the plural names (82%) are Meccan.

Say [O Muhammad!]: “Work! Allah will see your work, and so will His Messenger and the believers. You will then be returned to the One who knows the unseen and the visible and He will tell you what you were doing.”

(Qur’an, 9.105)

7

Categorization of the Meanings of the Chapter Names

The meanings of the names of the Qur'anic chapters may be grouped into seven categories each of which represents a particular theme. This is not the only categorization system, as any such system is bound to be approximate.

1) Attributes of Allah (SWT): There are seven chapters in this category, and they are listed in Table 7.1. Only chapters 24 and 55 are Medinite.

Table (7.1): The seven chapters named after attributes of Allah (SWT)

No.	Name	Meaning
24	An-Nūr	The Light
35	Fāṭir	The Originator [of Creation]
40	Ghāfir	The Forgiver
55	Ar-Raḥmān	The Merciful
67	Al-Mulk	The Kingship
70	Al-Ma'ārij	The Ascents
87	Al-A'lā	The Most High

It is worth mentioning that the attributes of Allah (SWT) are very frequent in the Qur'an. The name "Allah" occurs 2557 time in the Qur'an.

2) The Qur'an: All seven chapters in this category were revealed in Mecca. This reflects the fact that this was a period during which the authority of the Qur'an and the message of Prophet Muḥammad were being established and enforced. These chapters are shown in Table 7.2.

Table (7.2): The seven chapters named after the Qur'an or followed immediately by the word "al-Qur'an"

No.	Name	Meaning
1	Al-Fātiḥah	The Opening [of the Book]
25	Al-Furqān	The Criterion
36	Yā Sīn	The two Arabic letters of "Yā'" and "Sīn"
38	Ṣād	Ṣ [letter]
41	Fuṣṣilat	In Detail
50	Qāf	Arabic letter Q
97	Al-Qadr	Predestination

Three of these names are separate letters. The three names with the definite article start with lunar letters, just like the word "Qur'an."

3) The hereafter: As shown in Table 7.3, there are 17 chapters in this category. That fifteen of these chapters are Meccans reflects the fact this was one of the main themes in the Meccan period.

Table (7.3): The 17 chapters named after the hereafter

No.	Name	Meaning
7	Al-A'rāf	The Heights or [The wall with] Elevations
39	Az-Zumar	The Groups
44	Ad-Dukhān	The Smoke
45	Al-Jāthiyah	The Kneeling

52	Aṭ-Ṭūr	The Mount
56	Al-Wāqi'ah	The Event [of the Day of Resurrection]
64	At-Taghābun	The Mutual Loss or Gain
69	Al-Ḥāqqah	The inevitable
75	Al-Qiyāmah	The Resurrection
78	An-Naba'	The Tiding
79	An-Nāzi'āt	Those that pluck out
81	At-Takwīr	Making [something] lose its light
82	Al-Infiṭār	The Splitting
84	Al-Inshiqāq	The Rending
88	Al-Ghāshiyah	The Overwhelming [One]
99	Az-Zalzalah	The Earthquake
101	Al-Qāri'ah	The Striking Hour

4) Creature types: There are three chapters that are named after the angels (37), jinn (72), and human beings (76). These are listed in Table 7.4.

Table (7.4): The three chapters named after creature types

No.	Name	Meaning
37	Aṣ-Ṣāffāt	Those Ranged in Ranks
72	Al-Jinn	The Jinn
76	Al-Insān	The Human Being

Chapters 37 and 72 are Meccan while chapter 76 (al-Insān) is Medinite.

5) **Prophets**: This category, which contains 38 chapters, may be divided into two subgroups.

5.1) **Prophet Muhammed's life**: there are 24 chapters in this subgroup, 11 of them are Meccans and 13 are Medinites. The fact that this many chapters are named after events in the Prophet's life is not surprising. He, after all, was the Prophet of the Qur'an and the model that Allah created for people to follow. Table (7.5) summarizes the properties of this subgroup.

Table (7.5): The 24 chapters named after the Prophet's life

No.	Name	Meaning
8	Al-Anfāl	The Spoils [of war]
17	Al-Isrā'	The Night Journey
20	Ṭa Hā	The two Arabic letters of Ṭ and H
33	Al-Aḥzāb	The Confederates
47	Muḥammad	Muḥammad
48	Al-Fatḥ	The Victory
49	Al-Hujurāt	The Apartments
58	Al-Mujādilah	The Woman who disputes
59	Al-Ḥashr	The Gathering
60	Al-Mumtaḥanah	The Women to be examined
61	Aṣ-Ṣaff	The Rank
65	At-Ṭalāq	The Divorce
66	At-Taḥrīm	The Prohibition
73	Al-Muzzammil	The enwrapped one [in the garment]

74	Al-Muddaththir	The covered one
80	'Abasa	He Frowned
90	Al-Balad	The City
94	Al-Inshirāḥ	The Expanding
98	Al-Bayyinah	The Clear Proof
105	Al-Fīl	The Elephant
106	Quraish	[The Tribe of] Quraish
108	Al-Kawthar	Abundance
110	An-Naṣr	The Help
111	Al-Masad	The Palm-Fibre

5.2) Prophets and Righteous people: The second subgroup, of 14 chapters, concerns mainly prophets other than Muḥammad. In addition to 7 chapters about prophets, it also includes chapter 3 which is named after the father of Mariam (Mary), 'Īsā's (Jesus') mother, the chapter that carries the name of Mariam (19), and the chapter of Luqmān (31), who was not a prophet but a wise man. There are also another four chapters named after miracles of prophets Mūsā (Moses) (2), 'Īsā (5) and Sulaimān (Solomon) (27). The fourth is the miracle of the people of the cave (18).

Three of the fourteen chapters are Medinite, (2), (3) and (5). It was in Mecca when the basics of Islam were first revealed. It is also where the fact that Prophet Muḥammad's message was a continuation of the message of the prophets before him was established.

Table (7.6): The fourteen chapters named after prophets and other righteous people

No.	Name	Meaning
2	Al-Baqarah	The Cow [from the life of Mūsā]
3	Āl 'Imrān	The Family of 'Imrān
5	Al-Mā'idah	The Table of Food [from the life of 'Īsā]
10	Yūnus	[prophet] Jonah
11	Hūd	[prophet] Hūd
12	Yūsuf	[prophet] Joseph
14	Ibrāhīm	[prophet] Ibraham
18	Al-Kahf	The Cave
19	Mariam	Mary [Mother of 'Īsā]
21	Al-Anbiyā'	The Prophets
27	An-Naml	The Ants [from the life of Sulaimān]
28	Al-Qaṣaṣ	The Stories [from the life of Mūsā]
31	Luqmān	Luqman
71	Nūḥ	[prophet] Nūḥ

6) Life of the human being: There are 29 chapters in this group and can be divided into three subgroups. The chapter called "The Human Being" is included in the forth category of Creatures above.

6.1) Religious practices: This subgroup contains six chapters, three of which are Medinites (9, 22, and 62). These chapters are listed in Table (7.7).

Table (7.7): The six chapters named after religious practices and belief

No.	Name	Meaning
9	At-Tawbah	The Repentance
22	Al-Ḥajj	The Pilgrimage
32	As-Sajdah	The Prostration
42	Ash-Shūrā	The Consultation
62	Al-Jumu‘ah	Friday
112	Al-Ikhlāṣ	The Purity

6.2) Worldly Benefits: There are ten chapters in this subgroup, and only one of them is Medinite (57) (Table 7.8).

Table (7.8): The ten chapters named after worldly benefits

No.	Name	Meaning
6	Al-An‘ām	The Cattle
16	An-Naḥl	The Bees
29	Al-‘Ankabūt	The Spider
43	Az-Zukhruf	The Ornaments
57	Al-Ḥadīd	The Iron
68	Al-Qalam	The Pen
95	At-Tīn	The Figs
96	Al-‘Alaq	The Clots
100	Al-‘Ādiyāt	The Chargers
102	At-Takāthur	The Rivalry [by number]

Three chapters are names of animals and one means “cattle.” One chapter is named after a fruit (95), another after an element (57), a third after a tool (68), two refer to reproduction (96 and 102), and one is named after the ornaments of this world (43).

6.3) Groups of people: Thirteen chapters fall in this subgroup, and two of them are Medinites (4 and 63).

Table (7.9): The 13 chapters named after groups of people

No.	Name	Meaning
4	An-Nisa'	The Women
15	Al-Ḥijr	The Rocky Tract
23	Al-Mu'minūn	The Believers
26	Ash-Shu'arā'	The Poets
30	Ar-Rūm	The Romans
34	Saba'	[City of] Sheba
46	Al-Aḥqāf	The Sand-hills
63	Al-Munāfiqūn	The Hypocrites
83	Al-Muṭaffifīn	Those who give short measure
104	Al-Humazah	The Backbiter
107	Al-Mā'ūn	The Charity
109	Al-Kāfirūn	The Disbelievers
114	An-Nās	The People

7) Nature: There are 13 chapters in this category, and all of them, except chapter 13, are Meccans. This category can be divided into three subgroups.

7.1) Heavenly bodies: There are 5 chapters in this subgroup, all of them are Meccans. Table (7.10) lists the chapters in this group.

Table (7.10): The five chapters named after Heavenly bodies

No.	Name	Meaning
53	An-Najm	The Star
54	Al-Qamar	The Moon
85	Al-Burūj	The Constellations
86	Aṭ-Ṭāriq	The Night-Star
91	Ash-Shams	The Sun

7.2) Weather phenomena: There are three chapters in this subgroup two of them are Meccans (51 and 77). These chapters are listed in Table (7.11).

Table (7.11): The three chapters named after weather phenomena

No.	Name	Meaning
13	Ar-Ra'd	The Thunder
51	Adh-Dhāriyāt	The Scatterers
77	Al-Mursalāt	The Sent Ones

7.3) Times of the day: All five chapters in this category are Meccans. Table (7.12) lists these chapters.

Table (7.12): chapters named after times of the day

No.	Name	Meaning
89	Al-Fajr	The Dawn
92	Al-Layl	The Night
93	Aḍ-Ḍuḥā	The Forenoon
103	Al-'Aṣr	The Afternoon
113	Al-Falaq	The Daybreak

Table 7.13 summarizes the seven groups we have presented in this chapter.

Table (7.13): The number of chapters in each category

	Category's Title	Total
1	Attributes of Allah	7
2	The Qur'an	7
3	The hereafter	17
4	Creature types	3
5	Prophets	38
	5.1) Prophet Muhammed's life	24
	5.2) Prophets and Righteous people	14
6	Life of the human being	29
	6.1) Practices	6
	6.2) Worldly Benefits	10
	6.3) Groups of people	13
7	Nature	13
	7.1) Heavenly bodies	5
	7.2) Weather phenomena	3
	7.3) Times of the day	5

The most frequent category is that of the prophets (category number 5). The subcategory of Prophet Muḥammad's life contains the largest number of chapters, totalling 24. The second category is number 6 (Life of the human being) followed by the group of the hereafter (number 3) which contains 17 chapters.

8

The Chapters Listing

I will now list all Qur'anic chapters and study the verses from where their names were derived. I will give the following information about each chapter:

1. Its order in the muṣḥaf, i.e. in the written Qur'an.
2. The transliterated Arabic name and its meaning in English.
3. Whether it was revealed before the migration of the Prophet from Mecca (M) or after his *Hijrah* to Medina (H).
4. The Arabic text of verse in which the name is mentioned or from which it was derived. When the name occurs in more than one verse, only the first is quoted. The relevant word in the verse is highlighted in italics.
5. The English meaning of the verse and its number.
6. A short comment.

As mentioned in chapter 3, there are eight chapters with two names (5, 9, 17, 35, 40, 47, 65 and 76). Both names are mentioned in the heading of that section, and I have discussed both names.

The English translation of the Qur'anic verses is mine. I have used square brackets to provide further explanation.

1) Al-Fātiḥah (the Opening [of the Book]) (M)

This is one of the three chapters whose names are not found in exact or derivative form in their chapters (see chapter 4). Actually, the term "Fātiḥah" does not appear anywhere in the Qur'an.

Al-Fātiḥah means "The Opening," and its name is derived from the fact that it is the first chapter in the muṣhaf. This is why the Prophet referred to it as "The Fātīḥah of the Book" or "The Opening of the Book" in the ḥadīth we quoted earlier (see p. 14). Unlike any other chapter in the Qur'an, its *basmalah* is considered its first verse also.

Al-Fātiḥah is the most read chapter in Muslim prayers, as it must be recited at least 17 times a day in the five obligatory prayers. This chapter has also more than 20 descriptive names (see p. 18).

2) Al-Baqarah (The Cow) (H)

وَإِذْ قَالَ مُوسَى لِقَوْمِهِ إِنَّ اللَّهَ يَأْمُرُكُمْ أَنْ تَذْبَحُوا بَقَرَةً قَالُوا أَتَتَّخِذُنَا هُزُوًا قَالَ أَعُوذُ بِاللَّهِ أَنْ أَكُونَ مِنَ الْجَاهِلِينَ.

> And when Mūsā said to his people: Lo! Allah commands you that you sacrifice a *cow*, they said: Do you make game of us? He answered: I take refuge with Allah that I should be among the ignorant ones! (2.67)

The word *Baqarah* (cow) occurs in the story of a miracle whereby God revealed to Mūsā that some of his followers were trying to worship a cow and Allah ordered him to ask for it to be slaughtered. The term "cow" occurs in verses 68, 69, and 71 also, and its plural, "cows," is found in verse 70. All these verses are part of the story of that miracle. The plural form of the word is also found in verses 6.144, 6.146, 12.43, 12.46 but in different contexts from the story of the Mūsā' miracle.

3) Āl 'Imrān (The Family of 'Imrān) (H)

إِنَّ اللَّهَ اصْطَفَى آدَمَ وَنُوحًا وَآلَ إِبْرَاهِيمَ وَآلَ عِمْرَانَ عَلَى الْعَالَمِينَ.

Allah chose Adam, Nūḥ, the family of Ibrāhīm, and *the family of 'Imrān* above all nations. (3.33)

The verse in which the term *Āl 'Imrān* (family of 'Imrān) occurs starts a longer account of that noble family. Āl 'Imrān is mentioned only once in the Qur'an, but the word "'Imrān" is also mentioned in verse 35 in the expression "wife of 'Imrān."

The only other time in which the name 'Imrān is mentioned in the Qur'an is in verse 66.12 where Mariam is referred to as the "daughter of 'Imrān." So in total, the name 'Imrān is found three times in the Qur'an. The story of the family of 'Imrān, in the Qur'an, Christian writings, and historical sources is studied in detail in *The Mystery of the Historical Jesus: The Messiah in the Qur'an, the Bible, and Historical Sources* (Fatoohi, 2009).

Like other chapters, such as Ibrāhīm and Nūḥ, in which a dialog between a righteous person and Allah is mentioned, this chapter contains a conversation between the wife of Imrān and Allah (SWT).

The chapters of Āl 'Imrān and al-Baqarah are together called *az-Zahrāwān* (The Two Ever-Flowering).

4) An-Nisā' (The Women) (H)

يَا أَيُّهَا النَّاسُ اتَّقُوا رَبَّكُمُ الَّذِي خَلَقَكُم مِّن نَّفْسٍ وَاحِدَةٍ وَخَلَقَ مِنْهَا زَوْجَهَا وَبَثَّ مِنْهُمَا رِجَالًا كَثِيرًا وَنِسَاءً وَاتَّقُوا اللَّهَ الَّذِي تَسَاءَلُونَ بِهِ وَالْأَرْحَامَ إِنَّ اللَّهَ كَانَ عَلَيْكُمْ رَقِيبًا.

> O mankind! Be pious to your Lord who created you from a single soul, and from which He created its mate, and from the two of them He spread a multitude of men and *women*. Be pious to Allah in whom you claim [your rights] of one another and honor your ties of blood. Lo! Allah is a watcher over you. (4.1)

The exact word *Nisā'* (women) is also mentioned in the following 15 verses: 3, 4, 7, 11, 19, 22, 24, 32, 34, 43, 75, 98, 127 (twice), 129, and 176. The derivative word *nisā'ikum* (your women) is mentioned in verse 15 and 23 twice. This makes a total of 20 times in the chapter.

The word *Imra'ah* (woman) which is the singular of Nisā', is mentioned in verse 128. The word *Nisā'* and its derivatives are mentioned over 50 times in many other chapters.

Women related issues are one of the main themes in this chapter. They include women's rights and rulings about inheritance, marriage, divorce, and others.

5) Al-Mā'idah (The Table of Food) or al-'Uqūd (The Agreements) (H)

إِذْ قَالَ الْحَوَارِيُّونَ يَا عِيسَى ابْنَ مَرْيَمَ هَلْ يَسْتَطِيعُ رَبُّكَ أَنْ يُنَزِّلَ عَلَيْنَا مَائِدَةً مِنَ السَّمَاءِ قَالَ اتَّقُوا اللَّهَ إِنْ كُنتُمْ مُؤْمِنِينَ.

> When the companions said: "O 'Īsā, son of Mariam! Is your Lord able to send down for us a *table of food* from heaven? He said: "Be pious to Allah, if you are true believers." (5.112)

The exact word *Mā'idah* (table of food) is also mentioned in verse 114, in the same account of a miracle of the prophet 'Īsā when his companions asked him to make a table spread with food descend from heaven. This word is not mentioned elsewhere in the Qur'an.

This chapter is also called *al-'Uqūd* (the agreements or indentures):

يَا أَيُّهَا الَّذِينَ آمَنُوا أَوْفُوا بِالْعُقُودِ.

> O you how believe! Fulfil *the agreements*. (from 5.1)

Of the sources I quoted in this study (p. 18), only al-Ghazālī and as-Suyūṭī mention this name. The word *al-'uqūd* (the agreements or indentures) is mentioned only once in the Qur'an.

6) Al-An'ām (The Cattle) (M)

وَجَعَلُوا لِلَّهِ مِمَّا ذَرَأَ مِنَ الْحَرْثِ وَالأَنْعَامِ نَصِيبًا فَقَالُوا هَذَا لِلَّهِ بِزَعْمِهِمْ وَهَذَا لِشُرَكَائِنَا فَمَا كَانَ لِشُرَكَائِهِمْ فلا يَصِلُ إِلَى اللَّهِ وَمَا كَانَ لِلَّهِ فَهُوَ يَصِلُ إِلَى شُرَكَائِهِمْ سَاءَ مَا يَحْكُمُونَ.

> They (the polytheists) assign to Allah a share of the crops and *cattle* which He created, saying: "This is Allah's" — in their [false] claim — "and this [share] is for the partners we have with Him." Thus, that which they assign to His partners does not reach Allah, and that which they assign to Allah goes to their partners. Evil is their judgment. (6.136)

The word *an'ām* (cattle) is also mentioned in verses 138 (three times), 139, and 142. The word appears in other chapters 19 times, but its highest number of appearances in any one chapter is in this chapter where it is found 6 times. It appears in the context of explaining Islamic laws and benefits of cattle to people.

7) Al-A'rāf (The Heights or [The wall with] Elevations) (M)

وَبَيْنَهُمَا حِجَابٌ وَعَلَى الأَعْرَافِ رِجَالٌ يَعْرِفُونَ كُلاً بِسِيمَاهُمْ وَنَادَوْا أَصْحَابَ الْجَنَّةِ أَنْ سَلاَمٌ عَلَيْكُمْ لَمْ يَدْخُلُوهَا وَهُمْ يَطْمَعُونَ.

> Between them there is a veil. And on *the Heights* are men who know them all by their marks. And they call to the

dwellers of the Garden: "Peace be on you!" They have not entered it, for all their eagerness. (7.46)

The word *A'rāf* (Heights) is also mentioned in verse 48. This term is not found elsewhere in the Qur'an. The name refers to those who, after assessing their work on the Day of Judgment, will end up on the Heights between Hell and Paradise. They are able to see and speak to the dwellers of both adobes, while seeking Allah's mercy to take them to Paradise.

8) Al-Anfāl (The Spoils [of war]) (H)

يَسْأَلُونَكَ عَنْ الأَنْفَالِ قُلْ الأَنْفَالُ لِلَّهِ وَالرَّسُولِ فَاتَّقُوا اللَّهَ وَأَصْلِحُوا ذَاتَ بَيْنِكُمْ وَأَطِيعُوا اللَّهَ وَرَسُولَهُ إِنْ كُنتُمْ مُؤْمِنِينَ.

They ask you [O Muḥammad!] about the *spoils of war*. Say: "*The spoils of war* belong to Allah and the Messenger, so be pious to Allah, settle your differences, and obey Allah and His Messenger, if you are [true] believers. (8.1)

The word *anfāl* (spoils of war) is not found elsewhere in the Qur'an. It is the first topic in chapter 8.

9) At-Tawbah (The Repentance) or Al-Barā'ah (The Immunity) (H)

أَلَمْ يَعْلَمُوا أَنَّ اللَّهَ هُوَ يَقْبَلُ التَّوْبَةَ عَنْ عِبَادِهِ وَيَأْخُذُ الصَّدَقَاتِ وَأَنَّ اللَّهَ هُوَ التَّوَّابُ الرَّحِيمُ.

Don't they know that Allah does accept *repentance* from His servants and takes the alms, and that Allah is the Relenting, the Compassionate. (9.104)

The word *tawbah* (repentance) is mentioned once in verse 104 in this chapter. It occurs four times in the Qur'an, in 4.17, 4.18, and 42.25 in addition to the verse above. The attribute of Allah (SWT) *Tawwāb* is mentioned twice in this chapter (104, 118) and another 9 times in other chapters of the Qur'an.

بَرَاءَةٌ مِنَ اللَّهِ وَرَسُولِهِ إِلَى الَّذِينَ عَاهَدتُّم مِّنَ الْمُشْرِكِينَ.

Immunity [is given] from Allah and His messenger to those of the polytheists with whom you have made a treaty. (9.1)

This is one of the eight chapters that have two names. The second name, *barā'ah* (immunity), is the first word in the chapter. The verse gives the idolaters who did not enter a peace treaty with the Muslims immunity for four months. The term *barā'ah* is mentioned again in the Qur'an in 54.43.

It is worth mentioning that this is the only chapter that does not start with *basmalah* (p. 4).

10) Yūnus ([prophet] Jonah) (M)

فَلَوْلاَ كَانَتْ قَرْيَةٌ آمَنَتْ فَنَفَعَهَا إِيمَانُهَا إِلاَّ قَوْمَ يُونُسَ لَمَّا آمَنُوا كَشَفْنَا عَنْهُمْ عَذَابَ الْخِزْيِ فِي الْحَيَاةِ الدُّنْيَا وَمَتَّعْنَاهُمْ إِلَى حِينٍ.

If only there had been a community [of all those that were destroyed] that believed and profited from its belief as did the people of *Yūnus*! When they believed We removed from them the torment of disgrace in the life of this world and gave them comfort for a while. (10.98)

The name of prophet *Yūnus* (Jonah) is also met in 4.163, 6.86 and 37.139. Other details about his story are found in 37.139-148.

11) Hūd ([prophet] Hūd) (M)

وَإِلَى عَادٍ أَخَاهُمْ هُودًا قَالَ يَاقَوْمِ اعْبُدُوا اللَّهَ مَا لَكُمْ مِنْ إِلَهٍ غَيْرُهُ إِنْ أَنْتُمْ إِلاَّ مُفْتَرُونَ.

And to (the tribe of) 'Ād [We sent] their brother *Hūd*. He said: "O my people, worship Allah! You have no God other than Him. You are only forgers [of lies]. (11.50)

The name of prophet Hūd is also mentioned in another four verses in this chapter: 53, 58, 60, and 89. While prophet Hūd is mentioned in 7.65 and 26.124 also, there are more details in this chapter.

12) Yūsuf ([prophet] Joseph) (M)

إِذْ قَالَ يُوسُفُ لِأَبِيهِ يَاأَبَتِ إِنِّي رَأَيْتُ أَحَدَ عَشَرَ كَوْكَبًا وَالشَّمْسَ وَالْقَمَرَ رَأَيْتُهُمْ لِي سَاجِدِينَ.

When *Yūsuf* said to his father: "O my father! I saw eleven stars, the sun, and the moon; I saw them prostrating to me" (12.4)

The name of prophet Yūsuf (Joseph) is mentioned in another 24 times in the same chapter. Yūsuf is also mentioned in another two chapters: 6.84 and 40.34.

The story of Yūsuf is the only story that is mentioned in its entirety in the one chapter that carries his name. For a modern detailed study of the chapter of Yūsuf, see *The Prophet Joseph in the Qur'an, the Bible, and History* (Fatoohi, 2005).

13) Ar-Ra'd (The Thunder) (H)

وَيُسَبِّحُ الرَّعْدُ بِحَمْدِهِ وَالْمَلائِكَةُ مِنْ خِيفَتِهِ وَيُرْسِلُ الصَّوَاعِقَ فَيُصِيبُ بِهَا مَنْ يَشَاءُ وَهُمْ يُجَادِلُونَ فِي اللَّهِ وَهُوَ شَدِيدُ الْمِحَالِ.

The thunder proclaims His praise, and so do the angels for awe of Him. He sends the thunderbolts and smite with them whom He wills, while they dispute [in doubt] about Allah, and He is mighty in power. (13.13)

The word *ra'd* (thunder), which is mentioned only once in this chapter, occurs also in 2.19. Hence it is in the category of chapters that are mentioned last in their chapters (see chapter 4 and Table (4.3)).

14) Ibrāhīm ([prophet] Abraham) (M)

وَإِذْ قَالَ إِبْرَاهِيمُ رَبِّ اجْعَلْ هَذَا الْبَلَدَ آمِنًا وَاجْنُبْنِي وَبَنِيَّ أَنْ نَعْبُدَ الأَصْنَامَ.

When *Ibrāhīm* said: "My Lord! Make safe this territory, and preserve me and my sons from serving idols." (14.35)

The name of prophet Ibrāhīm (Abraham) is mentioned 70 times in 25 different chapters before and after this chapter. It is mentioned only once in this chapter with the famous prayer of Ibrāhīm for the future of Mecca, his son Ismā'īl (Ishmael), and his descendants. Like other chapters, such as Āl 'Imrān (3) and Nūḥ (71), this chapter contains a direct conversation between Ibrāhīm and Allah (SWT).

15) Al-Ḥijr (The Rocky Tract) (M)

وَلَقَدْ كَذَّبَ أَصْحَابُ الْحِجْرِ الْمُرْسَلِينَ.

And the dwellers of *the rocky tract* denied the messengers. (15.80)

The term *ḥijr* (rocky tract) is mentioned only in this verse. It is about a people who used to build their houses from rock and did not believe the prophets who were sent to them. They were seized by the Cry in the morning.

16) An-Naḥl (The Bees) (M)

وَأَوْحَى رَبُّكَ إِلَى النَّحْلِ أَنِ اتَّخِذِي مِنَ الْجِبَالِ بُيُوتًا وَمِنَ الشَّجَرِ وَمِمَّا يَعْرِشُونَ.

And thy Lord inspired *the bee* [saying]: "Take as habitations the hills, the trees, and what they build." (16.68)

The word *Naḥl* (bee) is mentioned only in this verse. The verse describes Allah's guiding of the bees to where they build their beehives.

17) Al-Isrā' (The Night Journey) or Banī Isrā'īl (The Children of Isreal) (M)

سُبْحَانَ الَّذِي أَسْرَى بِعَبْدِهِ لَيْلاً مِنَ الْمَسْجِدِ الْحَرَامِ إِلَى الْمَسْجِدِ الأَقْصَى الَّذِي بَارَكْنَا حَوْلَهُ لِنُرِيَهُ مِنْ آيَاتِنَا إِنَّهُ هُوَ السَّمِيعُ الْبَصِيرُ.

Glorified be He who *carried* His servant *by night* from the Inviolable Mosque to the Far Mosque whose neighborhood We have blessed, that We might show him of Our signs! Lo! He is the Hearer, the Seer. (17.1)

The noun *Isrā'* (night journey) is derived from the verb asrā (carried by night). It does not occur elsewhere in the Qur'an. It is about the miracle of the night journey of Prophet Muḥammad.

وَآتَيْنَا مُوسَى الْكِتَابَ وَجَعَلْنَاهُ هُدًى لِبَنِي إِسْرَائِيلَ أَلاَّ تَتَّخِذُوا مِنْ دُونِي وَكِيلاً.

And We gave Mūsā the Book and made it a guidance to the *Children of Israel* [saying]: "Do not take for yourselves any guardian other than Me." (17.2)

The second name of this chapter, *Banī Isrā'īl* (the Children of Israel) appears in verses 2, 4, 101, and 102. It appears 40 times in the Qur'an, reminding the reader of the 40 nights of that Mūsā spent on the mountain (2.51 and 7.142) and the 40 years that the Children of Israel spent in the wilderness after leaving Egypt (5.26). For a detailed study of the story of Mūsā in the Qur'an, see our book *The Mystery of Israel in Ancient Egypt: The Exodus in the Qur'an, the Old Testament, Archaeological Finds, and Historical Sources* (Fatoohi & Al-Dargazelli, 2008).

Pickthall is the only translator of the five sources mentioned earlier who refers to this chapter with its second name. He does not mention the other name.

18) Al-Kahf (The Cave) (M)

أَمْ حَسِبْتَ أَنَّ أَصْحَابَ الْكَهْفِ وَالرَّقِيمِ كَانُوا مِنْ آيَاتِنَا عَجَبًا.

Or do you think that the People of *the cave* and the mountain are a wonder among Our signs? (18.9)

The word *kahf* (cave) is also mentioned in verses 10, 11, and 16. The derivative word *kahfihim* (their cave) occurs in verses 17 and 25. The total is, therefore, six, which is the number of the youths in the cave. The miracle of these youths and how God put them into deep sleep in the cave for 309 solar years, which equal to 300 lunar years, is mentioned in this chapter only.

19) Mariam (Mary [Mother of 'Īsā]) (M)

وَاذْكُرْ فِي الْكِتَابِ مَرْيَمَ إِذْ انتَبَذَتْ مِنْ أَهْلِهَا مَكَانًا شَرْقِيًّا.

And mention [O Muḥammad!] *Mariam* in the Book. When she withdrew from her family to an eastern place. (19.16)

The word Mariam is also mentioned in verse 27 of this chapter and in the expression *Ibn Mariam* (son of Mary) in verse 34. In the whole Qur'an, *Mariam* appears 11 times and 23 times in the expression *Ibn Mariam*. This chapter recounts Mariam's story from the annunciation when she was given the news that she was going to miraculously conceive and give birth to an equally miraculous son. The earlier part of the story of Mariam, which covers her birth and dedication to the worship of God and living in the temple, is found in chapter 3 of the Qur'an.

20) Ṭa Hā ([The two Arabic letters of "Ṭ" and "H"]) (M)

طه.

Ṭā Hā. (20.1)

This is one of the four chapters that are named after separate letters. The separate letter *Ṭā*, the 16th letter of the Arabic alphabet, appears among the separate letters at the beginning of chapters 26, 27, and 29. The separate letter *Hā*, the 26th letter of the Arabic alphabet, appears again in the combination of separate letters with which chapter 19 starts.

The exact combination *Ṭā Hā* is not mentioned anywhere else in the Qur'an. Al-Ghazālī argues, contrary to common belief, that "there is nothing in hadīth (the literature of the sayings and doing of the Prophet) that confirms that *Ṭā Hā* is one of the names of Prophet Muhammed" (al-Ghazālī, p. 333).

21) Al-Anbiyā' (The Prophets) (M)

This is one of the three chapters whose names are not derived from a specific word in the chapter. However, the term *anbiyā'* (prophets) appears five times in four chapters. The singular *nabī* (prophet) is found 74 times in the Qur'an.

The name of this chapter is derived from the fact that it mentions the names of as many as 15 prophets: Ibrāhīm, Lūṭ (Lot), Isḥāq (Isaac), Ya'qūb (Jacob), Nūḥ (Noah), Dāwūd (David), Sulaimān (Solomon), Ayyūb (Job), Ismā'īl (Ishmael), Idrīs, Dhū al-Kifl, Dhū an-Nūn, Zakariyyah (Zechariah), Yaḥyā (John), and 'Īsā, as well as Mariam. This account covers more than 40 verses (21.48-91). In chapter 6 (al-An'ām), 18 names of prophets are mentioned, but only some details about prophet Ibrāhīm are mentioned in ten verses (6.74-83). The other 17 prophets are mentioned only by names in two verses (6.84-86). It is worth noting that the names of 25 prophets are mentioned in the Qur'an.

22) Al-Ḥajj (The Pilgrimage) (H)

وَأَذِّنْ فِي النَّاسِ بِالْحَجِّ يَأْتُوكَ رِجَالاً وَعَلَى كُلِّ ضَامِرٍ يَأْتِينَ مِنْ كُلِّ فَجٍّ عَمِيقٍ.

And proclaim to people *the pilgrimage*. They will come to you on foot and on every lean camel. They will come from every deep ravine. (22.27)

The word *ḥajj* (pilgrimage) is also mentioned in another 10 verses in the Qur'an. It is mentioned last in this chapter. This is the only chapter that is named after one of the five pillars of Islam.

23) Al-Mū'minūn (The Believers) (M)

قَدْ أَفْلَحَ الْمُؤْمِنُونَ.

Successful indeed are *the believers*. (23.1)

The word *mu'minūn* (believers) and its derivatives are also mentioned in verses 38, 44, 58, and 74. Verses 2-11 describe various attributes of the believers. The word itself and its derivatives appear numerous times in the Qur'an.

24) An-Nūr (The Light) (H)

اللَّهُ نُورُ السَّمَاوَاتِ وَالأَرْضِ مَثَلُ نُورِهِ كَمِشْكَاةٍ فِيهَا مِصْبَاحٌ الْمِصْبَاحُ فِي زُجَاجَةٍ
الزُّجَاجَةُ كَأَنَّهَا كَوْكَبٌ دُرِّيٌّ يُوقَدُ مِنْ شَجَرَةٍ مُبَارَكَةٍ زَيْتُونِةٍ لاَ شَرْقِيَّةٍ وَلاَ غَرْبِيَّةٍ يَكَادُ
زَيْتُهَا يُضِيءُ وَلَوْ لَمْ تَمْسَسْهُ نَارٌ نُورٌ عَلَى نُورٍ يَهْدِي اللَّهُ لِنُورِهِ مَنْ يَشَاءُ وَيَضْرِبُ اللَّهُ
الأَمْثَالَ لِلنَّاسِ وَاللَّهُ بِكُلِّ شَيْءٍ عَلِيمٌ.

Allah is the *Light* of the heavens and the earth. The similitude of His *light* is as a niche which has a lamp. The lamp is in a glass. The glass is as if it were a shining star. (This lamp is) kindled from a blessed tree — an olive tree — neither of the East nor of the West, whose oil would almost shine even if no fire touched it. [It is] *light* upon *light*. Allah guides to His *light* whom He wills. And Allah strikes similitudes for people. Allah knows of everything. (24.35)

The word *nūr* (light) is mentioned five times in this verse, which is known as the "verse of light," as well as twice in verse 40. It also appears many times in other chapters, but it is mentioned most in this chapter. *An-Nūr* is one of the attributes of Allah (SWT).

25) Al-Furqān (The Criterion) (M)

تَبَارَكَ الَّذِي نَزَّلَ الْفُرْقَانَ عَلَى عَبْدِهِ لِيَكُونَ لِلْعَالَمِينَ نَذِيرًا.

> Blessed is He who has revealed to His servant the *Criterion* [of right and wrong] that he may be a warner to the peoples. (25.1)

The term *furqān* (criterion), which refers to the Qur'an, is mentioned once in this chapter, in the first verse, and another 6 times elsewhere in the Qur'an: 2.53, 185, 3.4, 8.29 (derivative), 8.41 (as the day of al-furqān), and 21.48. It last appearance is in this chapter.

26) Ash-Shu'arā' (The Poets) (M)

وَالشُّعَرَاءُ يَتَّبِعُهُمُ الْغَاوُونَ.

> As for the *poets*, the erring follow them. (26.224)

The word *shu'arā'* (poets) is mentioned only once in the Qur'an. The singular *shā'ir* (poet) is mentioned four times, whereas the noun *shi'r* (poetry) occurs only once in 36.69.

27) An-Naml (The Ants) (M)

حَتَّى إِذَا أَتَوْا عَلَى وَادِي النَّمْلِ قَالَتْ نَمْلَةٌ يَاأَيُّهَا النَّمْلُ ادْخُلُوا مَسَاكِنَكُمْ لاَ يَحْطِمَنَّكُمْ سُلَيْمَانُ وَجُنُودُهُ وَهُمْ لاَ يَشْعُرُونَ.

> Until when they reached the Valley of the *Ants*, an *ant* exclaimed: "O *ants*! Enter your dwellings lest Sulaimān and his armies unknowingly crush you." (27.18)

The word *naml* (ants) is mentioned twice in this verse and once in the singular. The verse recounts one of the miracles of prophet Sulaimān, which is his ability to hear ants, and other animals, communicate and understand their language.

28) Al-Qaṣaṣ (The Stories) (M)

فَجَاءَتْهُ إِحْدَاهُمَا تَمْشِي عَلَى اسْتِحْيَاءٍ قَالَتْ إِنَّ أَبِي يَدْعُوكَ لِيَجْزِيَكَ أَجْرَ مَا سَقَيْتَ لَنَا فَلَمَّا جَاءَهُ وَقَصَّ عَلَيْهِ الْقَصَصَ قَالَ لاَ تَخَفْ نَجَوْتَ مِنَ الْقَوْمِ الظَّالِمِينَ.

Then one of the two women came walking to him (Mūsā) shyly. She said: "My father is inviting you that he may reward you with a payment for watering our flock for us. Then, when he came to him and told him the *stories*, he said: "Do not fear. You have escaped from the wrongdoing people." (28.25)

The word *qaṣaṣ* (stories) is mentioned three times elsewhere (3.62, 7.176 and 12.3), and its derivatives appear eight times. It refers here to the meeting between prophet Mūsā and prophet Shu'aib of Midyan.

29) Al-'Ankabūt (The Spider) (M)

مَثَلُ الَّذِينَ اتَّخَذُوا مِنْ دُونِ اللَّهِ أَوْلِيَاءَ كَمَثَلِ الْعَنكَبُوتِ اتَّخَذَتْ بَيْتًا وَإِنَّ أَوْهَنَ الْبُيُوتِ لَبَيْتُ الْعَنْكَبُوتِ لَوْ كَانُوا يَعْلَمُونَ.

The likeness of those who choose patrons other than Allah is as the likeness of the *spider* when she takes for herself a house. The frailest of all houses is the *spider's* house, if they knew! (29.41)

The word *'ankabūt* (spider) does not appear elsewhere in the Qur'an.

30) Ar-Rūm (the Romans) (M)

غُلِبَتِ الرُّومُ.

The *Romans* have been defeated. (30.2)

The term *Rūm* (Romans) is mentioned only here. It occurs in the context of recounting a prophecy that the Qur'an makes about a victory by the Romans over their enemies after an earlier defeat.

31) Luqmān (M)

وَلَقَدْ آتَيْنَا لُقْمَانَ الْحِكْمَةَ أَنْ اشْكُرْ لِلَّهِ وَمَنْ يَشْكُرْ فَإِنَّمَا يَشْكُرُ لِنَفْسِهِ وَمَنْ كَفَرَ فَإِنَّ اللَّهَ غَنِيٌّ حَمِيدٌ.

And verily We gave *Luqmān* wisdom [saying]: "Give thanks to Allah." And whosoever gives thanks, he gives thanks for [the good of] his soul. And whosoever refuses, Allah is self-sufficient, praiseworthy. (31.12)

The name of the wise man Luqmān is also mentioned in verse 13. Several verses (12-19) in this chapter, or about one quarter of the whole chapter, are about Luqmān's advice to his son.

32) As-Sajdah (The Prostration) (M)

إِنَّمَا يُؤْمِنُ بِآيَاتِنَا الَّذِينَ إِذَا ذُكِّرُوا بِهَا خَرُّوا سُجَّدًا وَسَبَّحُوا بِحَمْدِ رَبِّهِمْ وَهُمْ لَا يَسْتَكْبِرُونَ.

The only ones who believe in Our revelations are those who when reminded of them, they fall down *prostrate* and proclaim the praise of their Lord, and they are not arrogantly proud. (32.15)

Like the chapter of al-Isrā' (17) and other nine chapters (see Table 4.1), the exact name of this chapter is not found in the chapter but is derived from another term. The latter, *sujjadan* (prostrate), appears only once in the middle of this 30-verse long chapter. Variations of this word are very frequent in the Qur'an, occurring around 70 times.

33) Al-Aḥzāb (The Confederates) (H)

يَحْسَبُونَ الأَحْزَابَ لَمْ يَذْهَبُوا وَإِنْ يَأْتِ الأَحْزَابُ يَوَدُّوا لَوْ أَنَّهُمْ بَادُونَ فِي الأَعْرَابِ يَسْأَلُونَ عَنْ أَنْبَائِكُمْ وَلَوْ كَانُوا فِيكُمْ مَا قَاتَلُوا إِلاَّ قَلِيلاً.

They think that *the Confederates* have not gone [for good]; and if *the Confederates* should come [again], they would wish they were with the wandering Arabs [in the desert], asking for the news about you. And if they were among you, they would fight only little. (33.20)

The term *aḥzāb* (confederates) appears three times in this chapter, twice in verse 20 and once in verse 22. It is also mentioned nine times elsewhere in the Qur'an. The singular case (*ḥizb*) is mentioned eight times and the dual case (*ḥizbayn*) is mentioned once.

Meccan polytheists and Medinate Jewish tribes laid siege to the Muslims in Median. The failure of the siege of this confederation was a turning point in the life of the Prophet (PBUH) and the Muslims. It was the last serious danger of extermination that the Muslim community faced.

34) Saba' ([City of] Sheba) (M)

لَقَدْ كَانَ لِسَبَإٍ فِي مَسْكَنِهِمْ آيَةٌ جَنَّتَانِ عَنْ يَمِينٍ وَشِمَالٍ كُلُوا مِنْ رِزْقِ رَبِّكُمْ وَاشْكُرُوا لَهُ بَلْدَةٌ طَيِّبَةٌ وَرَبٌّ غَفُورٌ.

There was indeed a sign for *Saba'* in their dwelling-place: Two gardens on the right hand and on the left, [as it was said to them]: "Eat of the provision of your Lord and give thanks to Him; a good land and a forgiving Lord" (34.15)

The name *Saba'* (Sheba) is mentioned once in this chapter and once in 27.15. Both chapters contain parts of the story of prophet Sulaimān. His story is also mentioned in other chapters, but no chapter is named after him.

35) Fāṭir (The Originator [of Creation]) and al-Malā'ikah (The Angels) (M)

الْحَمْدُ لِلَّهِ فَاطِرِ السَّمَاوَاتِ وَالأَرْضِ جَاعِلِ الْمَلائِكَةِ رُسُلاً أُولِي أَجْنِحَةٍ مَثْنَى وَثُلاثَ وَرُبَاعَ يَزِيدُ فِي الْخَلْقِ مَا يَشَاءُ إِنَّ اللَّهَ عَلَى كُلِّ شَيْءٍ قَدِيرٌ.

Praise belongs to God, *the Originator* of the heavens and the earth, who makes *the angels* His messengers, endued with wings, in twos, threes, or fours. He adds to creation what He Pleases. God has power over all things! (35.1)

Unlike the other eight chapters each of which has two names, both names of this chapter appear in the first verse. Al-Ghazālī calls it *Fāṭir* and does not mention the second name.

Fāṭir is one of the attributes of Allah (SWT) and appears only once in this chapter. It is mentioned six times in the whole Qur'an (6.14, 12.101, 14.10, 39.46 and 42.11).

The second name, *al-Malā'ikah* (the angels), also appears only once in this chapter, but it occurs 67 more times in the Qur'an before and after this chapter.

36) Yā Sīn (The two Arabic letters of "Yā'" and "Sīn") (M)

يس.

Yā' Sīn. (36.1)

This is one of the four chapters whose names consist of separate letters. The combination of separate letters *Yā'*, the last or 28th letter of the Arabic alphabet, and *Sīn*, the 12th letter of the Arabic alphabet, appears only in this chapter. The letter *Yā'* appears also in the combination of separate letters at the beginning of chapter 19, and the letter *Sīn* appears in the separate letters of four other chapters: 26, 27, 28, and 42.

Al-Ghazālī (p. 478) states that "'*Yā Sīn*' do not, as commonly assumed, denote a name of Prophet Muḥammad."

37) Aṣ-Ṣāffāt (Those Ranged in Ranks) (M)

وَالصَّافَّاتِ صَفًّا.

By the [angels] *ranged in ranks*. (37.1)

This is the only time the word *Ṣāffāt* ([angels] ranged in ranks) appears in the Qur'an. This is the first of 14 chapters each of which starts with an oath.

38) Ṣād (Ṣ [letter]) (M)

ص وَالْقُرْآنِ ذِي الذِّكْرِ.

Ṣād, by the Qur'an of the Remembrance. (38.1)

This is another chapter whose name is a separate letter. The word/letter *ṣad*, the 14th letter of the Arabic alphabet, is mentioned once only in this chapter as a separate letter, but it appears 28 times in other words in the chapter. It is also part of the separate letters of chapters 7 and 19.

39) Az-Zumar (The Groups) (M)

وَسِيقَ الَّذِينَ كَفَرُوا إِلَى جَهَنَّمَ زُمَرًا حَتَّى إِذَا جَاءُوهَا فُتِحَتْ أَبْوَابُهَا وَقَالَ لَهُمْ خَزَنَتُهَا أَلَمْ يَأْتِكُمْ رُسُلٌ مِنْكُمْ يَتْلُونَ عَلَيْكُمْ آيَاتِ رَبِّكُمْ وَيُنْذِرُونَكُمْ لِقَاءَ يَوْمِكُمْ هَذَا قَالُوا بَلَى وَلَكِنْ حَقَّتْ كَلِمَةُ الْعَذَابِ عَلَى الْكَافِرِينَ.

The disbelievers shall then be driven in *groups* to hell. When they arrive there, its gates will be opened and its keepers will say to them: "Did messengers from among your not come to you, reciting to you the verses of your Lord and warning you against this day of encounter of yours?" They shall say: "Yes, but the word of the chastisement has been realized against the disbelievers." (39.71)

The word *zumar* (groups) is also mentioned in verse 73 which describes how the groups of believers are led to paradise in contrast to the groups of disbelievers who are taken to hell.

40) Ghāfir (The Forgiver) or al-Mū'min (The Believer) (M)

غَافِرِ الذَّنْبِ وَقَابِلِ التَّوْبِ شَدِيدِ الْعِقَابِ ذِي الطَّوْلِ لاَ إِلَهَ إِلاَّ هُوَ إِلَيْهِ الْمَصِيرُ.

[Allah is] the *forgiver* of sin, the One who accepts repentance, the One who is stern in punishment, the Bountiful. There is no God save Him. To Him is the journeying. (40.3)

This is one of the eight chapters that have two names each. The word *ghāfir* (forgiver) appears only once in this chapter, but its derivatives are frequent in the Qur'an in the form of "*ghafūr*" (forgiver) and once as "*khayru al-ghāfirīn*" (best of the forgivers). It is one of the attributes of Allah (SWT). Pickthall does not mention this name of the chapter.

وَقَالَ رَجُلٌ مُؤْمِنٌ مِنْ آلِ فِرْعَوْنَ يَكْتُمُ إِيمَانَهُ أَتَقْتُلُونَ رَجُلاً أَنْ يَقُولَ رَبِّيَ اللَّهُ وَقَدْ جَاءَكُمْ بِالْبَيِّنَاتِ مِنْ رَبِّكُمْ وَإِنْ يَكُ كَاذِبًا فَعَلَيْهِ كَذِبُهُ وَإِنْ يَكُ صَادِقًا يُصِبْكُمْ بَعْضُ الَّذِي يَعِدُكُمْ إِنَّ اللَّهَ لاَ يَهْدِي مَنْ هُوَ مُسْرِفٌ كَذَّابٌ.

A man who was a *believer* from Pharaoh's people who concealed his faith said: "Will you kill a man for saying 'my Lord is Allah' when he has come to you with manifest proofs from your Lord? If he is a liar then his lie would be against him, and if he is truthful then some of what he has threatened you with would fall on you. Allah does not guide one who is an extravagant liar." (40.28)

The term *mū'min* (believer), which represents the second name of the chapter, is also mentioned in verse 40. The related expression *al-ladhī āmana* (the one who believed) is mentioned in verses 30 and 38. It is also mentioned 22 times in the masculine and 6 in the feminine in other chapters.

The noun, in different cases, is mentioned over 200 times in the Qur'an. While the verb *āmana* appears, in different cases, is mentioned more than 400 times.

Ibn Kathīr does not mention the second name of the chapter.

41) Fuṣṣilat (In Detail) (M)

كِتَابٌ فُصِّلَتْ آيَاتُهُ قُرْآنًا عَرَبِيًّا لِقَوْمٍ يَعْلَمُونَ.

A Scripture whose verses have been *expounded* as an Arabic Qur'an for people who have knowledge. (41.3)

The word *fuṣṣilat* (expounded) appears also in verse 44 of this chapter and in verse 11.3.

42) Ash-Shūrā (The Consultation) (M)

وَالَّذِينَ اسْتَجَابُوا لِرَبِّهِمْ وَأَقَامُوا الصَّلَاةَ وَأَمْرُهُمْ شُورَى بَيْنَهُمْ وَمِمَّا رَزَقْنَاهُمْ يُنْفِقُونَ.

And those who answer the call of their Lord, observe prayer, make their affairs a *matter of consultation* among themselves, and spend of what We have bestowed on them. (42.38)

The term *shūrā* (consultation) appears only in this verse in the Qur'an.

43) Az-Zukhruf (The Ornaments) (M)

وَزُخْرُفًا وَإِنْ كُلُّ ذَلِكَ لَمَّا مَتَاعُ الْحَيَاةِ الدُّنْيَا وَالآخِرَةُ عِنْدَ رَبِّكَ لِلْمُتَّقِينَ.

And *ornaments*. Yet all that is only a provision of the life of this world. And the Hereafter with your Lord is for the pious. (43.35)

The word *zukhruf* (ornaments) appears only once in this chapter, but it also occurs in 6.112, 10.24, and 17.93.

44) Ad-Dukhān (The Smoke) (M)

فَارْتَقِبْ يَوْمَ تَأْتِي السَّمَاءُ بِدُخَانٍ مُبِينٍ.

So watch [O Muḥammad!] for the day when the sky will produce visible *smoke*. (44.10)

The term *dukhān* (smoke) appears in 41.11 also. It refers to a warning sign to people.

45) Al-Jāthiyah (The Kneeling one) (M)

وَتَرَى كُلَّ أُمَّةٍ جَاثِيَةً كُلُّ أُمَّةٍ تُدْعَى إِلَى كِتَابِهَا الْيَوْمَ تُجْزَوْنَ مَا كُنْتُمْ تَعْمَلُونَ.

And you will see every nation *kneeling* — every nation summoned to its record. [It will be said to them]: "Today you shall be recompensed for what you used to do." (45.28)

The word *jāthiyah* (kneeling) appears only in this verse. It denotes the Day of Judgment when every nation is summoned to its record.

46) Al-Aḥqāf (The Sand-hills) (M)

وَاذْكُرْ أَخَا عَادٍ إِذْ أَنْذَرَ قَوْمَهُ بِالأَحْقَافِ وَقَدْ خَلَتِ النُّذُرُ مِنْ بَيْنِ يَدَيْهِ وَمِنْ خَلْفِهِ أَلاَّ تَعْبُدُوا إِلاَّ اللَّهَ إِنِّي أَخَافُ عَلَيْكُمْ عَذَابَ يَوْمٍ عَظِيمٍ.

And make mention [O Muḥammad!] of the brother of 'Ād when he warned his people of *the sand-hills* — and warners came and went before and after him — [saying]: "Do not worship other than Allah. I fear for you the torment of a tremendous Day." (46.21)

The word *aḥqāf* (sand-hills) appears in this verse only.

47) Muḥammad or al-Qitāl (The Fighting) (H)

وَالَّذِينَ آمَنُوا وَعَمِلُوا الصَّالِحَاتِ وَآمَنُوا بِمَا نُزِّلَ عَلَى مُحَمَّدٍ وَهُوَ الْحَقُّ مِن رَّبِّهِمْ كَفَّرَ عَنْهُمْ سَيِّئَاتِهِمْ وَأَصْلَحَ بَالَهُمْ.

As for those who believe, do good works, and believe in that which has been revealed to *Muḥammad* — and it is the truth from their Lord — He acquits them of their bad deeds and improves their state. (47.2)

The name "Muḥammad" appears also in 3.144, 33.40 and 48.29. The name "Aḥmad," which is a variation of "Muḥammad," occurs in 61.6 in a prophecy that prophet 'Īsā makes about the coming of Prophet Muḥammad.

وَيَقُولُ الَّذِينَ آمَنُوا لَوْلاَ نُزِّلَتْ سُورَةٌ فَإِذَا أُنزِلَتْ سُورَةٌ مُّحْكَمَةٌ وَذُكِرَ فِيهَا الْقِتَالُ رَأَيْتَ الَّذِينَ فِي قُلُوبِهِم مَّرَضٌ يَنظُرُونَ إِلَيْكَ نَظَرَ الْمَغْشِيِّ عَلَيْهِ مِنَ الْمَوْتِ فَأَوْلَى لَهُمْ.

And those who believe say: "If only a chapter is revealed!" But when a perfect chapter is revealed and *fighting* is mentioned in it, you see those in whose hearts there is a disease looking at you with the look of someone fainting to death. Therefore, it is better for them. (47.20)

The word *qitāl* (fighting) is mentioned 12 times before this chapter. This name of the chapter is not mentioned by Pickthall.

48) Al-Fatḥ (The Victory) (H)

إِنَّا فَتَحْنَا لَكَ فَتْحًا مُّبِينًا.

We have given you [O Muḥammad!] a manifest *victory*. (48.1)

The word *fatḥan* (victory) is also mentioned in verses 18 and 27 of the same chapter. It also appears a number of times before and after this chapter.

49) Al-Ḥujurāt (The Apartments) (H)

إِنَّ الَّذِينَ يُنَادُونَكَ مِنْ وَرَاءِ الْحُجُرَاتِ أَكْثَرُهُمْ لاَ يَعْقِلُونَ.

Those who call you [O Muḥammad!] from behind *the apartments* — most of them do not understand. (49.4)

The term *ḥujurāt* (apartments) is not mentioned elsewhere in the Qur'an. It refers to the apartments of the Prophet.

50) Qāf (Arabic letter Q) (M)

ق وَالْقُرْآنِ الْمَجِيدِ.

Qāf. By the Glorious Qur'an. (50.1)

This is one of the four chapters whose names consist of separate letters. The letter *Qāf*, the 21st letter of the Arabic alpahabet, also appears in the separate letters of chapter 42. This letter is the first letter of the word "Qur'an."

51) Adh-Dhāriyāt (The Scatterers) (M)

وَالذَّارِيَاتِ ذَرْوًا.

By *the scatterers* that scatter. (51.1)

Referring to the wind, the term *dhāriyāt* (scatterers) appears only in this verse. This name refers to the spreading of pollen by the wind or wind pollination. This chapter is among a group of 14 chapters that start with an oath, like the following two chapters, 52 and 53.

52) Aṭ-Ṭūr (The Mount) (M)

وَالطُّورِ.

By *the Mount*. (52.1)

The word *ṭūr* (mount) is mentioned in another nine verses: 2.63, 2.93, 4.154, 19.52, 20.80, 23.20, 28.29, 28.46 and 95.2. It refers to Mount Sinai where prophet Mūsā received the Torah Tablets from God.

53) An-Najm (The Star) (M)

وَالنَّجْمِ إِذَا هَوَى.

By *the star* when it falls. (53.1)

The word *najm* (star) occurs another 3 times (16.16, 55.6, and 86.3). The plural *nujūm* (stars) is mentioned 9 times in the Qur'an.

54) Al-Qamar (The Moon) (M)

اقْتَرَبَتْ السَّاعَةُ وَانْشَقَّ الْقَمَرُ.

The hour has drawn nigh and *the moon* has split. (54.1)

The word *qamar* (moon) is mentioned 26 more times 19 of them before this chapter and 7 times after it.

55) Ar-Raḥmān (The Merciful) (H)

الرَّحْمَنُ.

The *Raḥmān*. (55.1)

This is one of the attributes of God in the Qur'an. It is mentioned only once in this chapter, but it occurs another 47 times in the Qur'an before and after this chapter. It is also part of the *basmalah*: *bismi illāhi ar-Raḥmāni ar-Raḥīm* (in the name of Allah the Merciful the

Compassionate). While the term *raḥmān* is usually translated as "merciful," it is used in the Qur'an as a proper name, like the name "Allah."

56) Al-Wāqi'ah (The Event [of the Day of Resurrection]) (M)

إِذَا وَقَعَتِ الْوَاقِعَةُ.

When *the Event* happens. (56.1)

The term *wāqi'ah* (event) is also mentioned in verse 69.15. Two derivative words are mentioned in verses 1 and 2. The term *al-wāqi'ah* refers to the Day of Resurrection.

57) Al-Ḥadīd (The Iron) (H)

لَقَدْ أَرْسَلْنَا رُسُلَنَا بِالْبَيِّنَاتِ وَأَنْزَلْنَا مَعَهُمُ الْكِتَابَ وَالْمِيزَانَ لِيَقُومَ النَّاسُ بِالْقِسْطِ وَأَنْزَلْنَا الْحَدِيدَ فِيهِ بَأْسٌ شَدِيدٌ وَمَنَافِعُ لِلنَّاسِ وَلِيَعْلَمَ اللَّهُ مَنْ يَنْصُرُهُ وَرُسُلَهُ بِالْغَيْبِ إِنَّ اللَّهَ قَوِيٌّ عَزِيزٌ.

Verily, We have sent Our messengers with clear proofs, and revealed with them the Book and the Balance, that mankind might observe justice. And We sent down *iron*, wherein is great might and uses for mankind, so that Allah may know him who helps Him and His messengers, though unseen. Allah is powerful, mighty. (57.25)

The term *ḥadīd* (iron) is mentioned only once in this chapter and another five times in verses 17.50, 18.96, 22.21, 34.10, and 50.22. So it makes its last appearance in this chapter.

58) Al-Mujādilah (The Disputing Woman) (H)

قَدْ سَمِعَ اللَّهُ قَوْلَ الَّتِي تُجَادِلُكَ فِي زَوْجِهَا وَتَشْتَكِي إِلَى اللَّهِ وَاللَّهُ يَسْمَعُ تَحَاوُرَكُمَا

إِنَّ اللَّهَ سَمِيعٌ بَصِيرٌ.

> Allah has heard the saying of her that *disputes* with you [O Muḥammad!] about her husband, and complains to Allah. And Allah hears your conversation. Lo! Allah is hearer, knower. (58.1)

The noun *mujādilah* (disputing woman) is not found in the chapter, but it is derived from the verbal form. The verb is mentioned another 24 times in the Qur'an before this chapter. It makes its last appearance in this chapter.

59) Al-Ḥashr (The Gathering) (H)

هُوَ الَّذِي أَخْرَجَ الَّذِينَ كَفَرُوا مِنْ أَهْلِ الْكِتَابِ مِنْ دِيَارِهِمْ لِأَوَّلِ الْحَشْرِ مَا ظَنَنْتُمْ أَنْ يَخْرُجُوا وَظَنُّوا أَنَّهُمْ مَانِعَتُهُمْ حُصُونُهُمْ مِنَ اللَّهِ فَأَتَاهُمُ اللَّهُ مِنْ حَيْثُ لَمْ يَحْتَسِبُوا وَقَذَفَ فِي قُلُوبِهِمُ الرُّعْبَ يُخْرِبُونَ بُيُوتَهُمْ بِأَيْدِيهِمْ وَأَيْدِي الْمُؤْمِنِينَ فَاعْتَبِرُوا يَا أُولِي الأَبْصَارِ.

> It is He who expelled the disbelievers among the People of the Book from their dwellings at the first *gathering*. You did not think that they would leave, and they thought that their fortresses would defend them against Allah. Then Allah came to them from whence they had not reckoned, and He cast terror into their hearts as they destroyed their houses with their own hands, and the hands of the believers; therefore take heed, you who have eyes! (59.2)

The term *ḥashr* (gathering) is mentioned only in this chapter. Verbal forms of this term are mentioned nearly 40 times, before and after this chapter, in reference to the Day of Resurrection.

60) Al-Mumtaḥanah (The Examined Woman) (H)

يَاأَيُّهَا الَّذِينَ آمَنُوا إِذَا جَاءَكُمُ الْمُؤْمِنَاتُ مُهَاجِرَاتٍ فَامْتَحِنُوهُنَّ اللَّهُ أَعْلَمُ بِإِيمَانِهِنَّ فَإِنْ عَلِمْتُمُوهُنَّ مُؤْمِنَاتٍ فَلاَ تَرْجِعُوهُنَّ إِلَى الْكُفَّارِ لاَ هُنَّ حِلٌّ لَهُمْ وَلاَ هُمْ يَحِلُّونَ لَهُنَّ

وَآتُوهُمْ مَا أَنفَقُوا وَلَا جُنَاحَ عَلَيْكُمْ أَنْ تَنكِحُوهُنَّ إِذَا آتَيْتُمُوهُنَّ أُجُورَهُنَّ وَلَا تُمْسِكُوا
بِعِصَمِ الْكَوَافِرِ وَاسْأَلُوا مَا أَنفَقْتُمْ وَلْيَسْأَلُوا مَا أَنفَقُوا ذَلِكُمْ حُكْمُ اللَّهِ يَحْكُمُ بَيْنَكُمْ
وَاللَّهُ عَلِيمٌ حَكِيمٌ.

O you who believe! When believing women come to you as emigrants, *examine* them. Allah knows better about their faith. Then, if you find them to be believers, do not return them to the disbelievers. They are not permitted to the disbelievers, nor are the disbelievers permitted to them. Give the disbelievers what they have expended; and there is no fault in you to marry them when you have given them their dowries. Do not hold fast to the matrimonial ties of disbelieving women, and ask to be paid back what you have expended, and let them ask to be paid back what they have expended. That is Allah's judgment; He judges between you; and Allah is knowing, wise. (60.10)

The word *Mumtaḥanah* (examined woman) is not mentioned in the chapter. The name is derived from a verbal form of that noun. Another derived verb is mentioned in 49.3.

61) Aṣ-Ṣaff (The Rank) (H)

إِنَّ اللَّهَ يُحِبُّ الَّذِينَ يُقَاتِلُونَ فِي سَبِيلِهِ صَفًّا كَأَنَّهُمْ بُنيَانٌ مَرْصُوصٌ.

Lo! Allah loves those who fight for His cause *in ranks* as if they were a compact building. (61.4)

The term *ṣaffan* (in ranks) is mentioned only once in this chapter. It is also found in 18.48, 20.64, 37.1, and 78.38 and twice in 89.22. Another derivative occurs in 52.20 and 88.15.

62) Al-Jumu'ah (Congregation / Friday) (H)

يَاأَيُّهَا الَّذِينَ آمَنُوا إِذَا نُودِيَ لِلصَّلَاةِ مِنْ يَوْمِ الْجُمُعَةِ فَاسْعَوْا إِلَى ذِكْرِ اللَّهِ وَذَرُوا
الْبَيْعَ ذَلِكُمْ خَيْرٌ لَكُمْ إِنْ كُنتُمْ تَعْلَمُونَ.

O you who believe! When the call is made for the prayer of the day of *congregation*, hasten to Allah's remembrance and leave your trading. That is better for you, if you knew. (62.9)

The term *Jumu'ah*, which means "congregation," denotes a collective prayer that is performed on "Friday." It is mentioned only in this chapter.

63) Al-Munāfiqūn (The Hypocrites) (H)

إِذَا جَاءَكَ الْمُنَافِقُونَ قَالُوا نَشْهَدُ إِنَّكَ لَرَسُولُ اللَّهِ وَاللَّهُ يَعْلَمُ إِنَّكَ لَرَسُولُهُ وَاللَّهُ يَشْهَدُ إِنَّ الْمُنَافِقِينَ لَكَاذِبُونَ.

When *the hypocrites* come to you [O Muḥammad!] and say: "We bear witness that you are indeed the Messenger of Allah," and Allah knows that you are indeed His Messenger, and Allah bears witness that *the hypocrites* are truly liars. (63.1)

The word *munāfiqūn* (hypocrites), which appears twice in the first verse of this chapter, is also mentioned in verses 7 and 8. It appears another 28 times, five of them specifying both male and female hypocrites. It appears last in this chapter in the nominative case.

64) At-Taghābun (The Mutual Loss or Gain) (H)

يَوْمَ يَجْمَعُكُمْ لِيَوْمِ الْجَمْعِ ذَلِكَ يَوْمُ التَّغَابُنِ وَمَنْ يُؤْمِنْ بِاللَّهِ وَيَعْمَلْ صَالِحًا يُكَفِّرْ عَنْهُ سَيِّئَاتِهِ وَيُدْخِلْهُ جَنَّاتٍ تَجْرِي مِنْ تَحْتِهَا الْأَنْهَارُ خَالِدِينَ فِيهَا أَبَدًا ذَلِكَ الْفَوْزُ الْعَظِيمُ.

When He shall gather you for the Day of Gathering; that shall be *the Day of Mutual Loss or Gain*. And whosoever believes in Allah and does righteousness, Allah will acquit him of his evil deeds and admit him into gardens underneath which rivers flow, therein to dwell forever and ever; that is the mighty triumph. (64.9)

The word *taghābun* (mutual loss or gain) appears only in this verse.

65) Aṭ-Ṭalāq (The Divorce) or an-Nisā' aṣ-Ṣughrā (The shorter [chapter of] the Women) (H)

يَاأَيُّهَا النَّبِيُّ إِذَا طَلَّقْتُمُ النِّسَاءَ فَطَلِّقُوهُنَّ لِعِدَّتِهِنَّ وَأَحْصُوا الْعِدَّةَ وَاتَّقُوا اللَّهَ رَبَّكُمْ
لاَ تُخْرِجُوهُنَّ مِنْ بُيُوتِهِنَّ وَلاَ يَخْرُجْنَ إِلاَّ أَنْ يَأْتِينَ بِفَاحِشَةٍ مُبَيِّنَةٍ وَتِلْكَ حُدُودُ اللَّهِ وَمَنْ
يَتَعَدَّ حُدُودَ اللَّهِ فَقَدْ ظَلَمَ نَفْسَهُ لاَ تَدْرِي لَعَلَّ اللَّهَ يُحْدِثُ بَعْدَ ذَلِكَ أَمْرًا.

> O Prophet, when you [O believers!] *divorce* women, divorce them after they have reached their set period. Count the period, and fear Allah your Lord. Do not expel them from their houses nor let them go forth, except when they commit a manifest indecency. Those are Allah's bounds; whosoever trespasses the bounds of Allah wrongs himself. You do not know, perchance after that Allah will bring something new to pass. (65.1)

The term *ṭalāq* (divorce) is not mentioned in this chapter, but a verbal form of the word exists. The word *ṭalāq* appears in 2.227 and 2.229. Other derivatives appear another 11 times in the Qur'an.

The second name of *an-Nisā' aṣ-Ṣughrā* identifies the main theme of the chapter which is women. This theme covers two thirds of the chapter. The first word of the name of this chapter suggests that this chapter shares the same theme of the chapter of *an-Nisā'* (The Woman), and the second word in the name, *aṣ-Ṣughrā* (shorter), refers to the fact that this chapter (12 verses only) is considerably shorter than chapter 4 (175 verses).

The second name of this chapter is not mentioned by al-Ghazālī and as-Suyūṭī.

66) At-Taḥrīm (The Prohibition) (H)

يَاأَيُّهَا النَّبِيُّ لِمَ تُحَرِّمُ مَا أَحَلَّ اللَّهُ لَكَ تَبْتَغِي مَرْضَاةَ أَزْوَاجِكَ وَاللَّهُ غَفُورٌ رَحِيمٌ.

O Prophet! Why do you *prohibit* that which Allah has made lawful for you, seeking to please your wives? Allah is Forgiving, Compassionate. (66.1)

The term *taḥrīm* (prohibition) is derived from the verb *tuḥarrim* (prohibit) which occurs in the verse above. Various forms of this verb appear 40 times in the Qur'an with the last appearance being in this chapter.

67) Al-Mulk (The Kingdom) (M)

تَبَارَكَ الَّذِي بِيَدِهِ الْمُلْكُ وَهُوَ عَلَى كُلِّ شَيْءٍ قَدِيرٌ.

Blessed be He in whose hand is the *kingdom*, and He is mighty over all. (67.1)

The term *mulk* (kingdom) is mentioned another 9 times elsewhere in the Qur'an. The last mention is in this chapter.

68) Al-Qalam (The Pen) (M)

ن وَالْقَلَمِ وَمَا يَسْطُرُونَ.

Nūn. By the *pen* and what they write. (68.1)

The term *qalam* (pen) is mentioned in 96.4 also. This chapter is among a group of 14 chapters that start with an oath, like chapters, 51, 52 and 53.

69) Al-Ḥāqqah (The inevitable One) (M)

الْحَاقَّةُ.

The *Indubitable One*! (69.1)

The term *ḥāqqa* (indubitable / inevitable) is also mentioned in verses 2 and 3. It is not mentioned elsewhere in the Qur'an. This expression refers to the Day of Resurrection.

70) Al-Ma'ārij (The Ascents) (M)

مِنَ اللَّهِ ذِي الْمَعَارِجِ.

From Allah, the Lord of the *ascents.* (70.3)

A derivative of the term *ma'ārij* (ascents) is also mentioned in verse 4. Derivative terms also occur in three other verses in the Qur'an before this chapter.

71) Nūḥ ([prophet] Noah) (M)

إِنَّا أَرْسَلْنَا نُوحًا إِلَى قَوْمِهِ أَنْ أَنذِرْ قَوْمَكَ مِن قَبْلِ أَن يَأْتِيَهُمْ عَذَابٌ أَلِيمٌ.

We sent *Nūḥ* to his people [saying]: "Warn your people before the painful doom comes to them." (71.1)

This chapter is all about prophet Nūḥ (Noah) whose name is also mentioned in verses 21 and 26. The name of this prophet appears in another 40 places in the Qur'an before this chapter.

72) Al-Jinn (The Jinn) (M)

قُلْ أُوحِيَ إِلَيَّ أَنَّهُ اسْتَمَعَ نَفَرٌ مِّنَ الْجِنِّ فَقَالُوا إِنَّا سَمِعْنَا قُرْآنًا عَجَبًا.

Say [O Muḥammad!]: "It has been revealed to me that a company of the *jinn* gave ear, then they said: 'We have indeed heard a wonderful Qur'an.'" (72.1)

The term *jinn*, which denotes a special kind of creatures, is also mentioned in verses 5 and 6. It appears in another 15 times before this chapter. It makes its last appearance in this chapter.

73) Al-Muzzammil (The Enwrapped One [in the Garment]) (M)

يَاأَيُّهَا الْمُزَّمِّلُ.

O enwrapped one! (73.1)

The term *muzzammil* (enwrapped one) is found in this chapter only. It refers to Prophet Muḥammad.

74) Al-Muddaththir (The covered one) (M)

يَاأَيُّهَا الْمُدَّثِّرُ.

O covered one! (74.1)

The term *muddaththir* (covered one) is mentioned only in this chapter. It refers to Prophet Muḥammad.

75) Al-Qiyāmah (The Resurrection) (M)

لاَ أُقْسِمُ بِيَوْمِ الْقِيَامَةِ.

No, I swear by the Day of *Resurrection*. (75.1)

The term *qiyāmah* (resurrection) is also mentioned in verse 6. The word occurs 70 times in the Qur'an, the last two of which are in this chapter. It makes its last appearance in this chapter.

76) Al-Insān (The Human Being) or ad-Dahr (The Time) (H)

هَلْ أَتَى عَلَى الإِنسَانِ حِينٌ مِنَ الدَّهْرِ لَمْ يَكُنْ شَيْئًا مَذْكُورًا.

Has there come on *the human being* a period of *time* when he was a thing unremembered? (76.1)

Both names of this chapter come from its first verse. The term *insān* (human being) is also mentioned in verse 2. This term occurs another 63 times in the Qur'an, as well as 20 times in the plural *ins* (mankind or human beings).

The term *dahr* (time) appears also in 45.24.

77) Al-Mursalāt (Sent Ones) (M)

وَالْمُرْسَلَاتِ عُرْفًا.

By those *sent* in a series! (77.1)

The term *mursalāt* (sent ones) refers to the winds that are sent in succession for the benefit of people. It appears only once in the Qur'an.

78) An-Naba' (The Tiding) (M)

عَنِ النَّبَإِ الْعَظِيمِ.

About the mighty *tiding*. (78.2)

The term *naba'* (tiding) is mentioned only at the beginning of this chapter. Other derivative words are mentioned many times in the Qur'an. The mighty tiding refers to the Day of Resurrection.

79) An-Nāzi'āt (Those that pluck out) (M)

وَالنَّازِعَاتِ غَرْقًا.

By *those that pluck out* vehemently. (79.1)

The term *nāzi'āt* (those that pluck out) is mentioned only in this chapter. It denotes the angels who violently pull out the souls of the wicked.

80) 'Abasa (He Frowned) (M)

عَبَسَ وَتَوَلَّى.

He frowned and turned away. (80.1)

The word *'abasa* (he frowned) refers to an incident when the Prophet Muḥammad ignored a blind man (Abdullāh bin Umm Maktūm) who visited him as he was busy trying to convince important tribe leaders to embrace Islam. The verb *'abasa* also mentioned in 74.22.

81) At-Takwīr (Making [something] lose its light) (M)

إِذَا الشَّمْسُ كُوِّرَتْ.

When the sun is *made to lose its light.* (81.1)

The term *takwīr* (making [something] lose its light) is not found in this chapter but is derived from the verb *kuwwirat* (made to lose its light). Another form of this verb, *yukawwir*, is found twice in 39.5.

82) Al-Infiṭār (The Splitting) (M)

إِذَا السَّمَاءُ انفَطَرَتْ.

When the heaven is *split.* (82.1)

The term *infiṭār* (splitting) is derived from the verb *infaṭarat* (split) and appears only in this chapter. It refers to a sign of the Day of Resurrection.

83) Al-Muṭaffifīn (Those who give short measure) (M)

وَيْلٌ لِلْمُطَفِّفِينَ.

Woe to *those who give short measure.* (83.1)

The term *muṭaffifīn* (those who give short measure) is mentioned in this chapter only.

84) Al-Inshiqāq (The Rending) (M)

إِذَا السَّمَاءُ انشَقَّتْ.

When the heaven is *rent asunder.* (84.1)

The term *inshiqāq* (rending) is not mentioned in the chapter, but the name is derived from a verb that shares the same root. The verb also appears in 54.1, 55.37, and 69.16. The rending of the heaven is one event of the Day of Resurrection.

85) Al-Burūj (The Constellations) (M)

وَالسَّمَاءِ ذَاتِ الْبُرُوجِ.

By the heaven of *the constellations.* (85.1)

The term *burūj* (constellations) is also mentioned in verses 4.78, 15.16, and 25.61 before this chapter. It makes its last appearance in this chapter.

86) Aṭ-Ṭāriq (The Night-Star) (M)

وَالسَّمَاءِ وَالطَّارِقِ.

By heaven and the *night-star.* (86.1)

The word *aṭ-Ṭāriq* (night-star) is also mentioned in verse 2.

87) Al-A'lā (The Most High One) (M)

سَبِّحِ اسْمَ رَبِّكَ الأَعْلَى.

Praise the name of your Lord the *Most High.* (87.1)

The term *al-A'lā* (Most High) is one of Allah's beautiful

names. The word appears another three times in the Qur'an in reference to Allah; the last time after this chapter is in 92.20.

88) Al-Ghāshiyah (The Overwhelming One) (M)

هَلْ أَتَاكَ حَدِيثُ الْغَاشِيَةِ.

Have you received the story of the *Overwhelming one*? (88.1)

Al-Ghāshiyah (Overwhelming one) is also mentioned in 12.107 without the definite article. It refers to the Day of Resurrection.

89) Al-Fajr (The Dawn) (M)

وَالْفَجْرِ.

By the *dawn.* (89.1)

The term *fajr* (dawn) is mentioned another 5 times in the Qur'an. This chapter and the following four chapters are among a group of 14 chapters that start with an oath, like chapters, 51, 52 and 53.

90) Al-Balad (The City) (M)

لاَ أُقْسِمُ بِهَذَا الْبَلَدِ.

No, I swear by this *city.* (90.1)

The term *balad* (city), which refers to Mecca in this verse, is also mentioned in verse 2 and 12 more times in the Qur'an, five times in the feminine *balda* and nine times in the masculine *balad.*

91) Ash-Shams (The Sun) (M)

وَالشَّمْسِ وَضُحَاهَا.

By *the Sun* and its noonday brightness. (91.1)

The term *shams* (sun) is mentioned another 29 times in the Qur'an. It makes its last appearance in this chapter.

92) Al-Layl (The Night) (M)

وَاللَّيْلِ إِذَا يَغْشَى.

By *the night* as it covers. (92.1)

The term *layl* (night) appears 73 times in the Qur'an before and after this chapter.

93) Aḍ-Ḍuḥā (The noon) (M)

وَالضُّحَى.

By *the noon*. (93.1)

The term *ḍuḥā* (noon) occurs in 7.98 and 20.59 also. The term *ḍuḥāhā* (its noon) 79.29, 79.46, and 91.1.

94) Al-Inshirāḥ or Ash-Sharḥ (The Expanding) (M)

أَلَمْ نَشْرَحْ لَكَ صَدْرَكَ.

Have We not *expanded* your breast for you? (94.1)

The term *Inshirāḥ* (expanding) is derived from the verb *nashraḥ* (expand) in the verse above. Derivative words are mentioned four times before this chapter. The verse addresses Prophet Muḥammad.

95) At-Tīn (The Fig) (M)

وَالتِّينِ وَالزَّيْتُونِ.

By *the fig* and the olive. (95.1)

The term *tīn* (fig) is mentioned in this chapter only. This chapter is among a group of 14 chapters that start with an oath, like chapters, 51- 53 and 90-93.

96) Al-'Alaq (The Clots) (M)

خَلَقَ الإِنسَانَ مِنْ عَلَقٍ.

He created man from *clots*. (96.2)

The name *'alaq* (clots) is mentioned in the singular form of *'alaqa* five times before this chapter.

97) Al-Qadr (Predestination) (M)

إِنَّا أَنزَلْنَاهُ فِي لَيْلَةِ الْقَدْرِ.

We revealed it [the Qur'an] on the Night of *Predestination*. (97.1)

The term *qadr* (predestination) occurs in verses 2 and 3 also. Derivative words appear frequently in the Qur'an.

98) Al-Bayyinah (The Clear Proof) (H)

لَمْ يَكُنِ الَّذِينَ كَفَرُوا مِنْ أَهْلِ الْكِتَابِ وَالْمُشْرِكِينَ مُنفَكِّينَ حَتَّى تَأْتِيَهُمُ الْبَيِّنَةُ.

Those who disbelieve among the People of the Book and the polytheists were not going to abandon [refusing Islam] until the *clear proof* comes to them. (98.1)

The term *bayyinah* (clear proof) is found in verse 4 also. It occurs 17 times in the Qur'an before this chapter. It makes its last appearance in this chapter.

99) Az-Zalzalah (The Earthquake) (H)

إِذَا زُلْزِلَتِ الأَرْضُ زِلْزَالَهَا.

When Earth is shaken with its [final] *earthquake*. (99.1)

The term *zalzalah* (earthquake) is derived from the word *zilzālahā* (its earthquake). It is also found in 22.1 without the definite article. Other derivative words are mentioned three times before this chapter. It makes its last appearance in this chapter.

100) Al-'Ādiyāt (The Chargers) (M)

وَالْعَادِيَاتِ ضَبْحًا.

By the *snorting chargers*. (100.1)

The term *'ādiyāt* (chargers) is mentioned in this chapter only. Some scholars have suggested that it refers to horses and others to camels. The action attributed to these animals, which I have translated here as "snorting," is the subject of disagreement among scholars.

101) Al-Qāri'ah (The Striking Hour) (M)

الْقَارِعَةُ.

The *Calamity*! (101.1)

The term *qāri'ah* (striking hour) is also mentioned in verses 2 and 3. It occurs twice before this chapter. The term refers to the Day of Resurrection.

102) At-Takāthur (The Rivalry) (M)

أَلْهَاكُمُ التَّكَاثُرُ.

Increasing in number has kept you busy. (102.1)

The term *takāthur* (Increasing in number) appears also in 57.20. The disbelievers used to proudly point to the large areas occupied by the graves of their tribes to boast that they are were bigger than rival tribes.

103) Al-'Aṣr (The Afternoon) (M)

وَالْعَصْرِ.

By the *afternoon*. (103.1)

This term *'Aṣr* (afternoon) appears only once in the Qur'an. This chapter is among a group of 14 chapters that start with an oath, like chapters, 51- 53 and 90-93.

104) Al-Humazah (The Backbiter) (M)

وَيْلٌ لِكُلِّ هُمَزَةٍ لُمَزَةٍ.

Woe to every slandering *backbiter*. (104.1)

The word *Humazah* (backbiter) appears only once in the Qur'an.

105) Al-Fīl (The Elephant) (M)

أَلَمْ تَرَى كَيْفَ فَعَلَ رَبُّكَ بِأَصْحَابِ الْفِيلِ.

Have you not seen how your Lord dealt with the people of the *Elephant*? (105.1)

This is the only place where the word *fīl* (elephant) appears in the Qur'an. It refers to the failed attempt of the ruler of Yemen, Abrahah, to demolish Ka'abah in Mecca in 570 CE – the year of the birth of Prophet Muḥammad. Abrahah's army employed an elephant.

106) Quraish (M)

لِإِيلَافِ قُرَيْشٍ.

For the uniting of *Quraish*. (106.1)

The name *Quraish* appears only once in the Qur'an. It is the name of the tribe of Prophet Muḥammad.

107) Al-Mā'ūn (The Charity) (M)

وَيَمْنَعُونَ الْمَاعُونَ.

Yet refuse [to give] *charity*! (107.7)

The term *mā'ūn* (charity) is found only once in the Qur'an.

108) Al-Kawthar (Abundance) (M)

إِنَّا أَعْطَيْنَاكَ الْكَوْثَرَ.

We have given you *Abundance*. (108.1)

The term *kawthar* (abundance) appears only once in the Qur'an. The verse addresses Prophet Muḥammad.

109) Al-Kāfirūn (The Disbelievers) (M)

قُلْ يَاأَيُّهَا الْكَافِرُونَ.

Say [O Muḥammad!]: O *disbelievers*! (109.1)

The *kāfirūn* (disbelievers) and its derivatives occur frequently in the Qur'an.

110) An-Naṣr (The Help) (H)

إِذَا جَاءَ نَصْرُ اللَّهِ وَالْفَتْحُ.

When Allah's *triumph* and victory come. (110.1)

The word *naṣr* (triumph) and its derivatives are

mentioned frequently in the Qur'an. The verse addresses Prophet Muḥammad.

111) Al-Masad (The Palm-Fibre) (M)

فِي جِيدِهَا حَبْلٌ مِنْ مَسَدٍ.

On her neck a rope of *palm-fibre*. (111.5)

The word *masad* (palm-fibre), which is the last word of the chapter, appears only once in the Qur'an. The verse talks about the wife of Abū Lahab, 'Awrā' bint Ḥarb, whose nickname is Umm Jamīl. She was as aggressive as her husband in opposing the message of Prophet Muḥammad. She was a sister of Abū Sufyān who played a leading role in the hostility of the Arab polytheists to the new religion.

112) Al-Ikhlāṣ (The Purity) (M)

This is the third chapter whose name is not derived from a word in the chapter. The term *ikhlāṣ* is not found in the Qur'an. The verbal forms (e.g. 4.146) and nouns (e.g. 2.139) that share the same root exist.

The term *ikhlāṣ*, which means "purity" or "exclusiveness," summarizes the essence of Qur'anic theology as it emphasizes the oneness of God, the fact that He has no peer, and that worship should be purely made to him.

This chapter is the second most read after chapter 1, as is it often recited in the daily prayers.

113) Al-Falaq (The Daybreak) (M)

قُلْ أَعُوذُ بِرَبِّ الْفَلَقِ.

Say: "I seek refuge in the Lord of the *Daybreak*." (113.1)

The term *falaq* (daybreak) appears only once in the Qur'an, but the related term *fāliq*, which means "creator," is found in verses 6.95 and 6.96.

114) An-Nās (The People) (M)

قُلْ أَعُوذُ بِرَبِّ النَّاسِ.

Say: "I seek refuge in the Lord of *people*." (114.1)

The term *nās* (mankind) occur in verses 2, 3, 5, and 6 also. It occurs very frequently in the Qur'an.

9

Conclusion

The Qur'an is the constitution of Islam and its main source. Over the centuries, Muslim scholars meticulously studied in detail all aspects of this divine book. The names of the Qur'anic chapters are one subject that scholars have studied extensively.

Most Muslim scholars agree that the names of the Qur'anic chapters were identified by the Prophet by divine revelation and were well known during his life.

Of the 114 chapters, 8 have each two names. Some of these names are more widely used than others. Certain combinations of chapters are also given special names as, for example, in the case of chapters 2 and 3 which are known as "az-Zahrāwān" (The Two Ever-Flowering).

There are three chapters whose names are not found in exact or derivative form in their respective chapters. In another 11 cases, the exact name of the chapter is not found in the chapter but is clearly derived from a word in that chapter. The names of the remaining 100 chapters appear in their exact forms in their respective chapters.

As for the location of the names, the names of 64 chapters appear in the first verse of their respective chapters. In nine cases, the name represents a whole verse. 72% of the names appear in the first 10 verses of a chapter. 11% and 15% of the names are in the middle or near the end of the chapter, respectively.

The shortest name of a Qur'anic chapter is one letter; there are two such chapters. The longest names are seven letters long, which is the case with three chapters.

The most frequent number of letters is three and the average number of letters per chapter is four. Eighty six names are found in the singular form (a noun and one letter are considered singular) and 28 names in the plural forms.

The names of the Qur'anic chapters cover various meanings, and there are many ways to categorize them. I have presented one such system whereby I split the names into seven different categories, with three of these categories split into subgroups. The seven categories are: Attributes of Allah, the Qur'an, the hereafter, creature types, prophets, life of humans, and nature. The category with the highest frequency is that of the prophets consisting of 38 out of 114 (one third). The biggest subcategory is that of Prophet Muḥammad with 24 chapters or 21% of the whole Qur'an. The second highest category is that of humans with 29 out of 114 or about one quarter of the Qur'an, followed by the hereafter which consists of 17 chapter or 15% of the Qur'an.

This book has presented observations that may be useful for others who are looking to understand their meanings. It is a small contribution to the study of the treasures of the Qur'an.

References

'Alī, 'Abdullah Yūsuf (2009).*The Meaning of the Holy Qur'ān: Text, Translation and Commentary*, Islamic Book Trust: Kuala Lumpur.

Aḥmad ibn Ḥanbal, Abū 'Abdullah (Undated). *Musnad Aḥmad*, al-Shaybānī.

Al-Ghazālī, M. (2006). *A Thematic Commentary on the Qur'an*, Islamic Book Trust: Kuala Lumpur.

Al-Qattan, M. (1996). *Mabāḥith fī 'Ulūm al-Qur'ān*, Maktabah al-Ma'ārif: Riyadh.

As-Suyūṭī, Jalāl al-Dīn (Undated). *Al-Itqān fiī 'Ulūm al-Qur'ān*, vol. 1, Dār Maktabah al-Hilāl: Cairo.

At-Tirmidhi, Abū 'Īsā Muhammad (Undated). *Sunan al-Tirmidhī* (Undated). The Book of virtues of Qur'an (48), section on the virtue of the Qur'an, hadith number 2906.

Az-Zarqānī, Muḥammad (Undated). *Manāhil Al-'Irfan fī 'Ulūm al-Qur'ān* (The Springs of Knowledge of the Sciences of the Qur'an), Dār Iḥyā' al-Turāth al-'Arabī: Lebanon.

Bukhārī, Abū 'Abdullah Muhammad (1997). *Ṣaḥīḥ al-Bukhārī*, Riyadh.

Fatoohi, L (2005). *Prophet Joseph in the Qur'an, the Bible, and History*, Islamic Book Trust: Kuala Lumpur.

Fatoohi, L. & Al-Dargazelli, S. (2008). *The Mystery of Israel in Ancient Egypt: The Exodus in the Qur'an, the Old Testament, Archaeological Finds, and Historical Sources*, Luna Plena Publishing: UK.

Fatoohi, L. (2009). *The Mystery of the Historical Jesus: The Messiah in the Qur'an, the Bible, and Historical Sources*, Islamic Book Trust: Kuala Lumpur.

Fatoohi, L. (2010a). *The First Verse Of The Qur'an.*

http://www.quranicstudies.com/louay-fatoohi/quran/the-first-verse-of-the-quran.html.

Fatoohi, L. (2010b). *The Last Verse Of The Qur'an.* http://www.quranicstudies.com/louay-fatoohi/quran/the-last-verse-of-the-quran.html.

Fatoohi, L. (2010c). *The Difference Between "Qur'an" and "Muṣḥaf."* http://quranicstudies.com/louay-fatoohi/quran/the-difference-between-quran-and-mushaf.html.

Ibn Kathīr, Ismā'īl (1999). *Tafsīr al-Qur'ān al-'Aẓīm*, Dār Ṭībah lilnashr wa al-Tawzī': Riyadh.

Muṣḥaf al-Madīnah an-Nabawiyyah (1985). Al-Madīnah al-Munawwarah, Saudi Arabia.

Muslim, Abū al-Hussain (1990). *Ṣaḥīḥ Muslim*, Dār al-Kutub al-'Ilmiyyah, Beirut, Lebanon, 1st print, 1990.

Pickthall, M. M. (Undated). *The meaning of the Glorious Qur'an*, An explanatory translation, Albirr Foundation: UK.

Index of Names and Subjects

www.ingramcontent.com/pod-product-compliance
Lightning Source LLC
Chambersburg PA
CBHW020554030426
42337CB00013B/1101
* 9 7 8 1 9 0 6 3 4 2 0 8 1 *